THE PHILOSOPHUS GRADE WORK

of

PAUL FOSTER CASE

by Wade Coleman

I0172731

ACKNOWLEDGEMENTS

A special thank you to Dolores Ashcroft-Nowicki for permission to publish The Unreserved Dedication.

TABLE OF CONTENTS

COPYRIGHT SEARCH

United States Copyright Office
Library of Congress 101 Independence Avenue SE
Washington, DC 2055906000

August 1, 2025

Our reference:

Our search in the appropriate Copyright Office indexes and catalogs that include works cataloged from 1938 through July 1, 2025 under the names [B.O.T.A.], [Builders of the Adytum], and Paul Foster Case and the title THE BIRTH OF THE WORLD SAVIOR disclosed no separate registration for a work identified under these names and the specific title.

Our search in the appropriate Copyright Office indexes and catalogs that include works cataloged from 1978 through July 1, 2025 under the names L. W. and the titles THE DUTIES OF THE ARCHON, THE FIRE WAND, THE ROLE OF THE ARCHON, AND TASK OF THE PHILOSOPHUS disclosed no separate registration for a work identified under these names and the specific title.

Our search in the appropriate Copyright Office indexes and catalogs that include works cataloged from 1978 through July 1, 2025 under the names Paul Clark and the titles PORTAL ASSIGNMENTS and THE RITUAL OF THE FLAMING CUBE disclosed no separate registration for a work identified under these names and the specific title.

Our search in the appropriate Copyright Office indexes and catalogs that include works cataloged from 1978 through July 1, 2025 under the names Paul Clark and the titles PREPARATION TO PORTAL disclosed no separate registration for a work identified under these names under the specific title.

INTRODUCTION

I use abbreviations for the three main floor officers: EA, A-t, A-t and H-r. The C-n (Consecrator) and P-r (Purifier) are so easy to guess that I published these names in the text.

I use abbreviations for the three main floor officers: EA, A-t, A-t and H-r. The C-n (Consecrator) and P-r (Purifier) are so easy to guess that I published these names in the text. I substituted the Golden Dawn names: Praemonstrator, Imperator, and Cancellarius for the Grand Chief's names.

Manly P. Hall says, "The Lesser Mysteries are rituals of self-control and purification; the Greater Mysteries arc rituals of creation." He adds that Creation Mysteries are threefold: the creation of *form*, *thought* and *consciousness*. – *The Most Holy Trinosophia*, p. 89., Aziloth Books)

In the Zelator attunement ritual, it says:

> Be thou, therefore, prompt and active as the Sylphs, but avoid frivolity and caprice. Be energetic and strong like the Salamanders, but avoid irritability and ferocity. Be flexible and attentive to images, like the Undines, but avoid idleness and changeability. Be laborious and patient, like the Gnomes, but avoid grossness and avarice. So shalt thou gradually develop the powers of thy soul and fit thyself to command the spirits of the elements.

In a nutshell, this is the work of the first order.

This symbolism is apparent in the Golden Dawn first-order red shoes and black robes. Symbolically, shoes represent base desire. Red is the color of Mars. This symbolizes that the initiate's elemental nature is governed by their passions. In the second order, the elemental nature is purified, so the initiates wear yellow shoes that symbolize their base desires are under intelligent control.

The robe is the outer garment; astrologically, this is symbolized by the ascendant or personality. The change from black to white robes for advancement suggests the purification of the personality.

Alchemically, the Black Work is the putrefaction and decomposition, where the personality is broken down into its base elements. Following the chaos and confusion of the Black Work, the alchemist purifies their desires in the White Work.

Paul Case changed the symbolism. Why, I can only speculate.

Paul Case removed most references to pagan deities and Qlippoth from the Golden Dawn rituals. An online search shows that the term "Red Shoe Club" has two meanings. One is a charitable group that helps children, while the other red symbolism implies hiding the blood of their victims. Therefore, the red symbolism and black robes are not appropriate for Christian initiates.

In Case's order, the first order wears white shoes, and the second order is barefooted. Both the first and second orders wear white robes. Symbolically, the *white* shoes represent that our desires are purified or under God's (Kether) control. The white robes suggest the same of our personalities. Barefoot suggests the removal of base desires.

In his lessons, Case stresses the importance of habitually reminding yourself that all your actions and thoughts originate from God. To see God in everything, I call this the Saint's Path, the right-hand Pillar of Mildness with Chokmah, Chesed and Netzach.

The left-hand Pillar of Severity is Binah, Geburah and Hod. Although none of the sephirah or evil, the negative influences of Geburah and Mars loosely associate this with the left-hand path of pursuing passions.

Then, there is the Arrow's Path of the Masonic Blue Lodge. On the Tree of Life, the paths connecting the middle pillar are blue (Malkuth to Yesod is violet, which is the addition of a little red to blue). This is a Path of Service. All these paths are a way to attainment. However, they are not the Magician's Path of the flaming sword that touches all sephiroth.

If it were my choice, the initiate would wear the same color belt and shoes to symbolize their current grade. However, buying a different pair of shoes for each level isn't practical. Our order included shoes or socks (all white, no logo). I feel more grounded when I wear socks rather than shoes during rituals.

I offer this advice to those who desire to start a ritual group. Symbolism is important, and changing the ritual and regalia needs to be taken seriously.

The Elephant in the Room

Speaking of symbolism, the tablets are the fundamental change between the Golden Dawn rituals and Paul Case.

Our tablets were based on Hebrew. In *The Golden Dawn American Source Book*, Paul Case had nothing good to say about the Enochian Tablets in the Golden Dawn rituals.

I cannot comment on Enochian because I have never used the system. Many very smart people have spent time and effort building a correspondence of sound, color, and musical notes with Hebrew letters. This rich symbolism is excellent for magical work.

CHAPTER 1- Philosophus

THE TASK OF A PHILOSOPHUS

EA: Honored A-n, what does the Throne of the West symbolize?

A-n: Increase of darkness and decrease of light.

EA: Your duties?

A-n: I preside over the twilight and darkness encompassing us without the sun of life and light. I guard the gate of the West. I assist with the candidate's reception and superintend the subordinate officers in executing their duties.

The following is the minimum required to advance from the grade of 4=7 to the grade of 4=7 Senior. At least three months must pass between these grades. The Portal grade may only be conferred at the summer or winter solstice.

1.   Continue the daily performance of the Greater Water Ritual and the associated practices as described in the 3=8 instruction. Record the results of this and all other practices in your journal.

2.   Demonstrate, to the satisfaction of the examining Chief, the Ritual of the Flaming Cube. Note in your Journal the experiences derived from this ritual.

3.   Meditate on the various verses of the Chaldean Oracles, recording the results. The Ritual of the Flaming Cube should be used with these meditations. From this, select at least three meditations to hand in during your exam.

4.   During this period, give the Sign of a Philosophus when performing the daily salutations.

5.   Pass the written and oral examinations on the Knowledge Lecture. The oral portion must be taken, without references, in the presence of a Chief. **Do not submit this examination until you have completed all other tasks.**

4=7 Knowledge Lecture
The Azoth Lecture

1. Azoth is a word formed from the initial and final letters of the Latin, Greek and Hebrew alphabets: A, Z, Alpha and Omega, Aleph and Tav, thus:

$$A \ Z \ \Omega \ ת$$

Alchemical writers use it with many variant meanings. Still, its general significance is "Essence, Beginning and End, the Astral Light wherein are the elements and the philosophical Mercury extracted from the sun."

2. The Cross with equal arms usually represents the equation of the elements. In the planetary symbols, this cross also signifies corrosion or resolution into parts.

3. *Arikh Anpin* (אריך אנפין). Macroprosopus, or Vast Countenance, is a title of Kether, the first Sephirah. It is also known as *Auttiq Yomin* (עתיק יומין), the Ancient of Days.

Arikh Anpin is conformed into Chokmah and Binah, Father and Mother, Ab (אב) and Aima (אימא).

These two, united, are *Elohim* (אלהים) and are the parents of *Zauir Anpin* (זעיר אנפין), Microprosopus, the Lesser Countenance. *Zauir Anpin* is also known as Adam (אדם), the essential being of the entire human race, as Melek (מלך), the King, and as Ben (בן), the Son.

To *Zauir Anpir* are attributed the six Sephiroth: Chesed, Geburah, Tiphareth, Netzach, Hod and Yesod. Of these, the special Sephirah attributed to Zauir Anpin, or the Sephirah in which Melek Adam, the Son, is seated, is the sixth Sephirah, Tiphareth.

4. *Malkah* (מלכה), the Queen, and Kallah (כלה), the Bride, are titles of Malkuth, considered as the spouse of Microprosopus.

5. The four letters of Tetragrammaton (יהוה) are thus attributed:

י   to Chokmah or Ab, the Supernal Father;

ה   to Binah or Aima, the Supernal Mother;

ו   to Zauir Anpin, Microprosopus;

ה   final, to Malkuth.

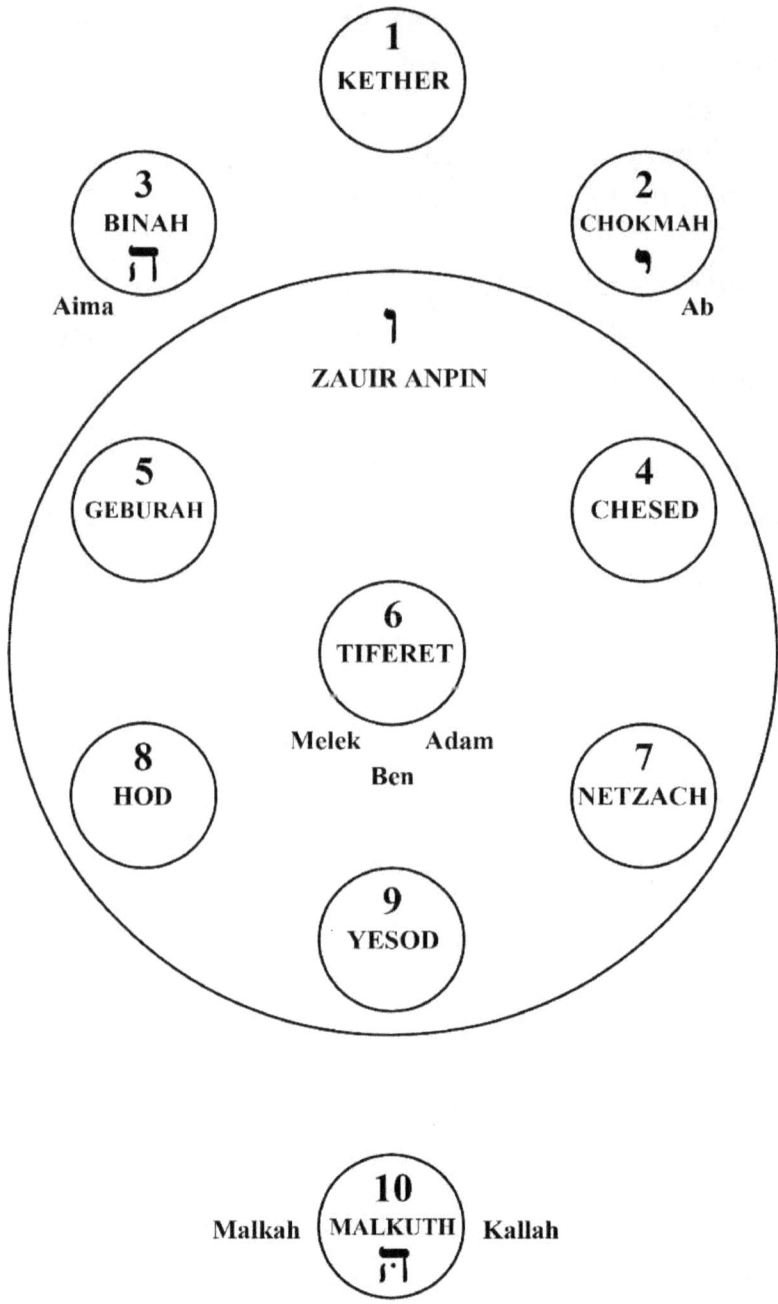

These letters refer to the four worlds and the four suits of Tarot:

י	Atziluth	Wands	Fire
ה	Briah	Cups	Water
ו	Yetzirah	Swords	Air
ה	Assiah	Pentacles	Earth

6. In each of the four worlds are the ten Sephiroth of that world, and each Sephirah has its own ten Sephiroth, making 400 Sephiroth in all – the number of Tav, the Cross, the Universe, the Completion of all things.

7. The Secret Names of the four worlds are:

Atziluth	Aub	עב	72
Briah	Seg	סג	63
Yetzirah	Mah	מה	45
Assiah	Ben	בן	52

They are the totals of the numbers of the letters of Tetragrammaton when spelled in full in the four worlds, as follows:

Atziluth	הי	ויו	הי	יוד	72
Briah	הי	ואו	הי	יוד	63
Yetzirah	הא	ואו	הא	יוד	45
Assiah	הה	וו	הה	יוד	52

15

8. Each of the twenty-two connecting paths of the Tree of Life (the paths of the twenty-two Hebrew letters) represents the equilibrium of the two Sephiroth it joins.

9. The arrangement of the ten Sephiroth, as given in the *Sepher Yetzirah*, or *Book of Formation*, is as follows:

Kether	כתר	Ruach Elohim	רוח אלהים	Spirit
Chokmah	חכמה	Aveer	אויר	Air
Binah	בינה	Maim Eretz	מים ארץ	Water Earth
Chesed	חסד	Aesh	אש	Fire

These four constitute the tetrad of the elements.

5	Geburah	גבורה	HEIGHT
6	Tiphareth	תפארת	EAST
7	Netzach	נצח	SOUTH
8	Hod	הוד	NORTH
9	Yesod	יסוד	DEPTH
10	Malkuth	מלכות	WEST

These six constitute the hexad of the dimensions of space, symbolized by the Cube of Balanced Forces.

10. The ten Sephiroth are thus united into Seven Palaces:

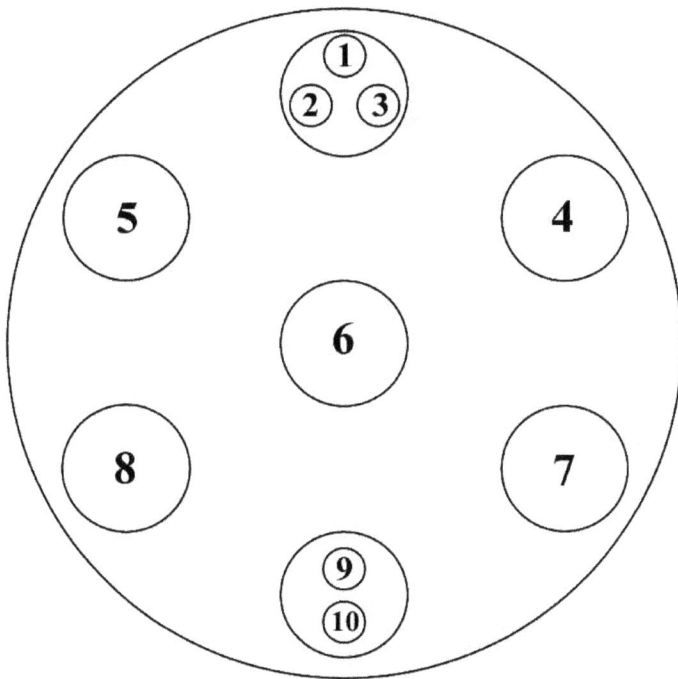

11. The Calvary Cross of Twelve Squares, the Admission Badge of the twenty-ninth path of Qoph, symbolizes the zodiac and the eternal River of Eden, divided into four parts.

	Nahar The River	נהר
1	Hiddekel	הדקל
2	Pison	פישון
3	Gihon	גיחון
4	Phrath	פרת

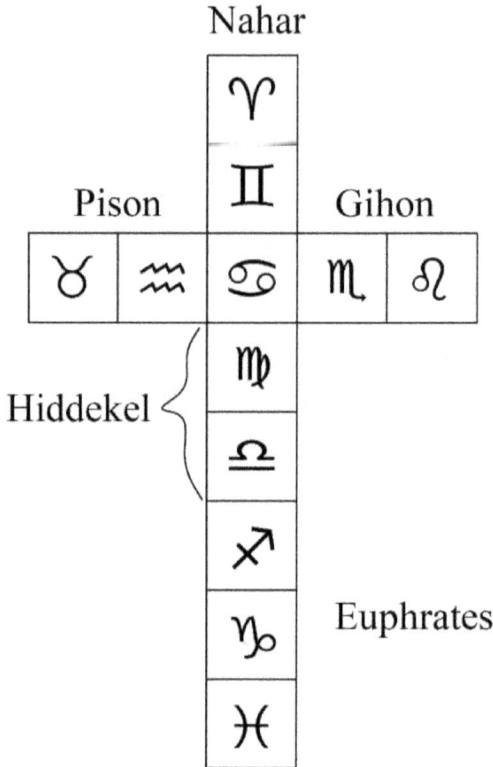

Nahar

Pison   Gihon

Hiddekel

Euphrates

18

12. The Cube of Balanced Forces, the Admission Badge of the twenty-eighth path of the letter Tzaddi, symbolizes the six dimensions of space. Its meaning is based on the following passage from the Sepher Yetzirah, or Book of Formation:

He sealed the Height, turned toward Above, and sealed it with יהו.

He sealed the Depth, turned toward Below, and sealed it with והי.

He sealed the East, turned forward, and sealed it with היו.

He sealed the West, turned backward, and sealed it with ויה.

He sealed the North, turned to the right, and sealed it with הוי.

He sealed the South, turned to the left, and sealed it with יוה.

The first trigram, *Yeho* (יהו), is attributed to Height in the translations of the *Sepher Yetzirah*. *Yeho* is a Hebrew name of God, said by Gesenius as a shorter form of the Tetragrammaton (יהוה). This three-letter name appears as a compound in many Hebrew proper names. We may think of it as either a short form of Tetragrammaton or a longer form of Jah (יה), the special designation of God in *The Book of Formation*.

Chapter 1, Section 1 *Sepher Yetzirah* says Jah is *high, elevated*, and *dwelling on high*. Compare these statements with the Qabalistic attribution of Jah to Chokmah, the Sphere of the Zodiac, or "Highway of the Stars." Consequently, it is appropriate to attribute *Yeho* (יהו) to the Height where God abides.

No published text of the *Sepher Yetzirah* assigns the trigram (והי) to Depth, but it will be seen that the order of its letters is the reverse of that in (יהו). This practice of reversing the letters of a word to indicate an opposite meaning is characteristic of the Qabalah. Since Depth is the opposite of Height, it is evident that the oral teaching on which this instruction is based is correct when it assigns to Depth the trigram (והי).

In the Mantua Codex of the *Sepher Yetzirah*, one of the oldest, and in Stenring's translation, the trigram (היו) is assigned, as above, to the direction East. *Mizrach* (מזרח), East, is properly "the place of sunrise." The noun is derived from a verb which signifies "to rise, to break forth," and is thus definitely connected with the ideas of *source* or *origin*. Therefore, the trigram (היו) is assigned to it, which is the infinitive absolute of the Hebrew verb meaning "to be." This trigram denotes a simple "being," the source of all modes of manifestation.

The fourth trigram (ויה) is assigned to the direction West. Note that it is the reverse of the trigram attributed to the East. Furthermore, because it is a verbal construction expressing the future, "shall be" (ויה) corresponds logically to West, for West, as the place

20

of sunset, represents the completion of a time cycle, and since we are at present amid an uncompleted "day of manifestation," the end of this cycle is yet in the future, and is "what shall be." In confirmation of this, we may note that the noun *Ma'arab* (מערב) also means "evening."

The trigram (הוי) is assigned to the North because the North is the direction corresponding to the hidden forces, which are the powers employed in practical occultism. In this connection, note that North (in Section 9 of this lecture) is attributed to Hod, the Sphere of Mercury and that Mercury or Hermes is the god of magic. In Hebrew, the basic meaning of *Tzaphon* (צפון), North, is "the hidden region." The direction of the hidden forces is an expression of conscious intention. The trigram expresses this (הוי), the imperative, "Be thou."

The sixth trigram (יוה) is the reverse of (הוי) and is attributed to the South in the translations and versions of Loria, Saadya Gaon and Kalisch. It expresses the reverse of what is represented by (יוה) because the direction South, as the place of the sun's greatest meridian height, corresponds to the state of full enlightenment, in which there is neither need for nor exercise of the imperative mood. The Hebrew name for South, Darom (דרום), confirms this, derived from a root that signifies "to glance, to sparkle, to radiate."

21

13. The Calvary Cross of Ten Squares refers to the ten Sephiroth in balanced disposition. It is also the open form of the Double Cube and the Altar of incense:

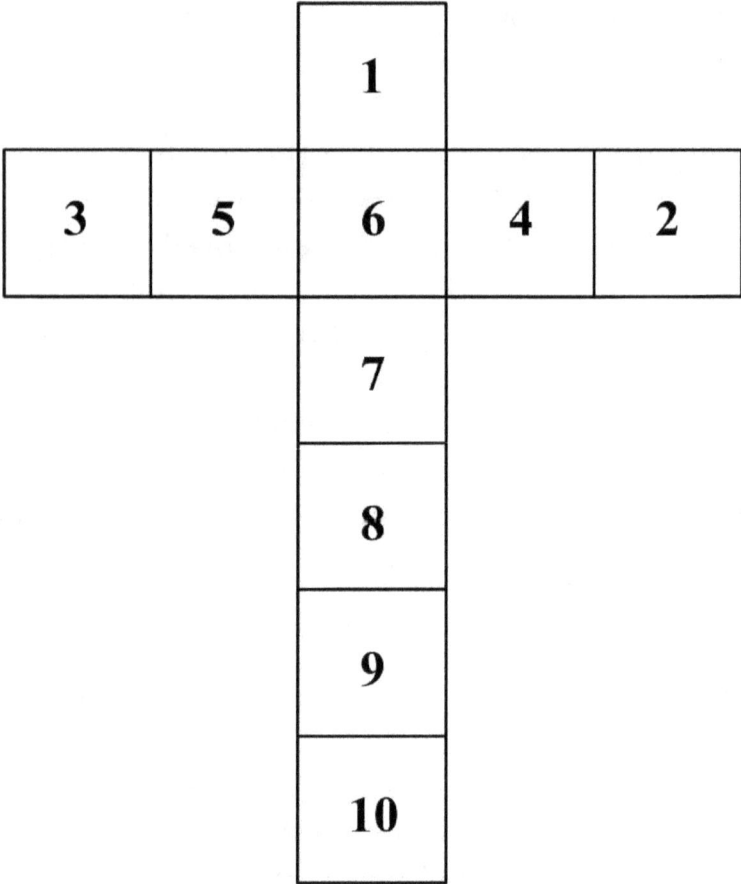

		1		
3	**5**	**6**	**4**	**2**
		7		
		8		
		9		
		10		

14. The following diagram refers to the Trinity operating through the Sephiroth and reflected downward in the four triangles of the elements:

Trinity on the Tree of Life

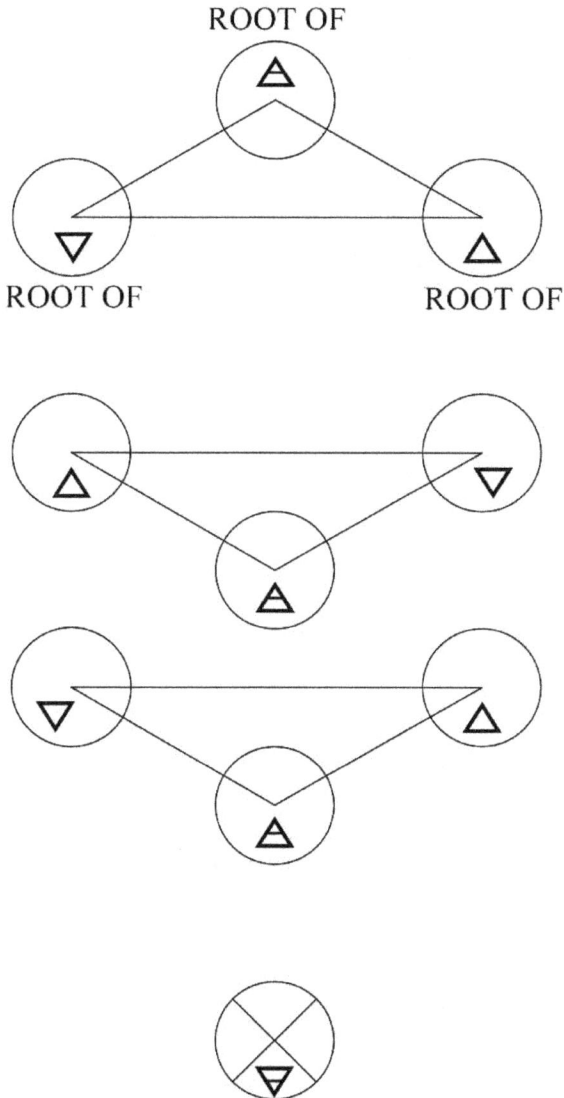

ROOT OF

ROOT OF   ROOT OF

Kether is the Root of Air, reflected downward from Kether to Yesod through Tiphareth.

Chokmah is the Root of Fire, reflected from Chokmah, through Geburah, to Netzach.

Binah is the Root of Water, reflected from Binah through Chesed to Hod.

The tenth Sephirah Malkuth is Earth, the receptacle and synthesis of Air, Fire and Water.

END OF THE AZOTH LECTURE

* * *

Examination: 4 = 7 to PORTAL

Answer the following questions orally:

1. To what element is the twenty-ninth path attributed?

2. What Sephiroth does it join?

3. What is the Admission Badge of this path?

4. To what element is the twenty-eighth path attributed?

5. What Sephiroth does it join?

6. What is the Admission Badge of the twenty-eighth path?

7. To what element and to what planet is the twenty-seventh path attributed?

8. What Sephiroth does it join?

9. What is the Admission Badge of this path?

10. To what element is the Grade of Philosophus attributed?

11. Of what planet is this Grade the Sphere?

12. What is the Admission Badge of this Grade?

13. What is the Grand Word of 4 = 7? What is the Mystic number? What is the password? Give the Mystic Title and its meaning. What is the symbol of this Grade? What title of respect is attached to this Grade? What further symbol belongs to it?

14. Perform, to the satisfaction of the examining Chief, the Ritual of the Flaming Cube.

Answer the following questions in writing:

The Grades from Zelator to Philosophus inclusive correspond to four fields of human endeavor, each having its specific type of work, in which the advancing Initiate should endeavor to make himself as proficient as possible. Sufficient indications of this have been given in the Rituals and Lectures. State, as briefly as is consistent with clarity, what your understanding of these fields of endeavor and the work appropriate to each may be.

Several types of Crosses are used in the First Order. Name them, with the Grades and paths to which they are attributed, and give your explanation of (1) why the general symbol of the *Cross* is employed, (2) the relation of each Cross to the type of personal endeavor toward spiritual unfoldment which characterizes the paths in which those Crosses are symbols.

Now that you have attained the highest Grade of the First Order, what is your conception of the proper relation of an Initiate:

(1) to the Life-power;
(2) to the Order and its members;
(3) to humanity, in general.

Explain how the Trinity of Elements manifests on the Tree of Life.

Give three examples of meditations performed on the Chaldean Oracles.

CHAPTER 2 – Shem Ha-Mephorash

The 72 Names from Exodus

By MacGregor Mathers
Edited by Paul Clark

Four is the number of the letters in the name Jehovah (יהוה). Four is also the number of the letters in the Name Adonai (אדני), which serves as its substitute and key. The latter name is linked to the former, uniting them thus:

יאהדונהי

Multiplying 8 by 3 (the number of the Supernal Triad) results in the 24 Thrones of Wisdom, the 24 Thrones of the Elders of the Apocalypse, each wearing a golden crown with three rays. Each ray represents a name; each name is an absolute idea and the ruling power of the Great Name Tetragrammaton (יהוה).

The number 24 of the Thrones multiplied by the three rays of the crown equals 72. The name of God with 72 letters is thus mystically represented in the Name IHVH, as the Book of Revelations states: "When the living creatures (the four Kerubim, the letters of the Name) give glory, etc., to Him, etc., the four and twenty Elders fall before Him and cast their crowns before the Throne. (That is the crowns, which each bear 3 of the 72 names. These 72 names are written on the leaves of the Tree of Life, which were for the healing of the nations.

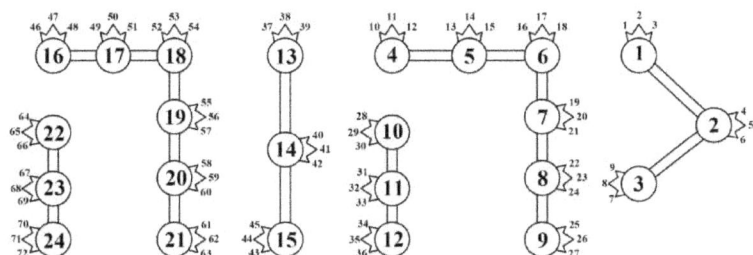

These are also the 72 rounds of the ladder of Jacob on which the angels of God ascended and descended. The 72 angelic names are formed from the 72 names of the Deity, which are derived from the 19th, 20th, and 21st verses of the 14th chapter of the Book of Exodus.

Exodus 14:19: The angel of God, traveling before Israel's army, withdrew and went behind them. The pillar of the cloud also moved from in front and stood behind them.

va.Yisa (ויסע) – then he withdrew

Mal'akh ha.Elohim (מלאך האלהים) — the angel of God

ha.Holekh (ההלך) – traveling

Lifnei (לפני) – before

Machaneh Yisra'el (מחנה ישראל) – the army of Israel

va.Yelekh (וילך) – and he went

Me'achareihem (מאחריהם) – behind them

va.Yisa (ויסע) – and moved

'Amud ha.'Anan (עמוד הענן) – the pillar of cloud

Mipneihem (מפניהם) – from before them

va.Ya'amod (ויעמד) – and stood

Me'achareihem (מאחריהם) – behind them

29

Exodus 14:20: Coming between the armies of Egypt and Israel. Throughout the night, the cloud brought darkness to one side and light to the other side, so neither went near the other all night long.

va.Yavo (ויבא) – and it came
Bein (בין) – between
Machaneh (מחנה) – the army of
Mitzrayim (מצרים) – Egypt
u.Vein (ובין) – and between
Machaneh (מחנה) – the army of
Yisra'el (ישראל) – Israel

va.Yehi (ויהי) – and it came to pass
ha,'anan (הענן) – the cloud
ve.ha.Choshekh (והחשך) – and the darkness
va.Yor (ויאר) – and he gave light
Et ha-laylah (את הלילה) – the night

Ve.lo (ולא) – and not, neither
Karav (קרב) – came near, approached
Zeh (זה) – this one
El (אל) – to, toward
Zeh (זה) – the other

(neither came near the other)

Kol ha.laylah (כל הלילה) – all the night

Exodus 14:21 And Moses stretched out his hand over the sea, and all night the Lord drove the sea back with a strong east wind and turned it into dry land, and the waters were divided.

va.Yet (ויט) – then he stretched

Mosheh (משה) – Moses

Et yado (את ידו) – his hand

'Al (על) – over

ha.Yam (הים) – the sea

va.Yolekh (ויולך) – and he drove back

YHWH (יהוה) – Yahweh, the Lord

Et ha.yam (את ידו) – the sea

b'Ruach (ברוח) – with a wind

kadim (קדים) – of the east

'Azah (עזה) – strong

Kol ha.laylah (כל הלילה) – all the night

Vayasem (וישם) – and he turned

Et ha.yam (את ידו) – the sea

le.Charavah (לחרבה) – into dry land

va.Yibake'u (ויבקעו) – and they were divided

Ha.mayim (המים) – the waters

These three verses should be written one above the other: the first (19th) from right to left, the second (20th) from left to right, and the third (21st) from right to left. Each verse contains 72 letters, creating 72 columns with three letters each. Each column represents a word of three letters, the Shem ha-Mephorash, or 72 Names of the Deity, illustrating the Powers of the Name.

The 72 names are arranged in four columns with 18 names each. Each column is associated with one of the letters of the Tetragrammaton and the four Cabalistic Worlds.

V19	כ	ל	ה	ה	מ	י	ה	ל	א	ה	כ	א	ל	מ	ע	ס	י	ו
V20	ל	א	ק	ר	ב	ז	ה	א	ל	ז	ה	כ	ל	ה	ל	י	י	ה
V21	י	ו	מ	י	ה	ל	ע	ו	ד	י	ת	א	ה	ש	מ	ט	י	ו
	18	17	16	15	14	13	12	11	10	9	8	7	6	5	4	3	2	1

V19	מ	כ	ל	י	ו	ל	א	ר	ש	י	ה	נ	ח	מ	י	נ	פ	ל
V20	נ	ו	ה	ח	ש	כ	ו	י	א	ר	א	ת	ה	ל	י	ל	ה	ו
V21	ד	ק	ח	ו	ר	ב	מ	י	ה	ת	א	ה	ו	ה	י	כ	ל	ו
	36	35	34	33	32	31	30	29	28	27	26	25	24	23	22	21	20	19

V19	נ	נ	ע	ה	ד	ו	מ	ע	ע	ס	י	ו	מ	ה	י	ר	ח	א
V20	י	נ	מ	ח	נ	ה	י	ש	ר	א	ל	ו	י	ה	י	ה	ע	נ
V21	ת	א	מ	ש	י	ו	ה	ל	י	ל	ה	ל	כ	ה	ז	ע	מ	י
	54	53	52	51	50	49	48	47	46	45	44	43	42	41	40	39	38	37

V19	מ	ה	י	ר	ח	א	מ	ד	מ	ע	י	ו	מ	ה	י	נ	פ	מ
V20	ו	י	ב	א	ב	י	נ	מ	ח	נ	ה	מ	צ	ר	י	מ	ו	ב
V21	מ	י	מ	ה	ו	ע	ק	ב	י	ו	ה	ב	ר	ח	ל	מ	י	ה
	72	71	70	69	68	67	66	65	64	63	62	61	60	59	58	57	56	55

From these 72 names of angels, some are formed by adding the name Yah (יה), which signifies Mercy and Beneficence, while others incorporate El (אל), representing Severity and Judgment. As it is said, "And the Name is in him." (Exodus 23:21)

These 72 Names govern the 72 quaternaries or groups of 5 degrees of the Zodiac. Therefore, each decan or 10-degree segment of a sign has two quaternaries, and each sign has three decanates, which are again assigned to the planets in a regular order.

Hebrew is written from right to left. For these tables, I wrote the Hebrew from left to right.

Shem ha-Mephorash Attributions

PRESIDENCY – י

1st Choir – Seraphim			
#	God Name		Angelic Name
1	והו	הי	Vahaviah
2	ילי	לא	Yelayiel
3	סיט	לא	Saitel
4	מלע	הי	Olmiah
5	שהמ	הי	Mahashiah
6	הלל	לא	Lelahel
7	אכא	הי	Akaiah
8	תהכ	לא	Kehethel

2nd Choir – Kerubin			
9	יזה	לא	Haziel
10	דלא	הי	Aldaiah
11	ואל	הי	Laviah
12	עהה	הי	Hihaayah
13	לזי	לא	Yeyalel
14	הבם	לא	Mebahael
15	ירה	לא	Harayel
16	מקה	הי	Hoqamiah

3rd Choir – Thrones			
17	ואל	הי	Laviah
18	ילכ	לא	Keliel

3rd Choir – Thrones			

19	וול	הי	Livohyah
20	להפ	הי	Phehilyah
21	כלנ	לא	Nelokhiel
22	ייי	לא	Yeyayiel
23	הלמ	לא	Melohel
24	והח	הי	Chahaviah

4th Choir – Dominions			
25	התנ	הי	Nithahiah
26	אאה	הי	Haeyoh
27	תרי	לא	Yirthiel
28	האש	הי	Sahayoh
29	ייר	לא	Reyayel
30	מוא	לא	Evamel
31	בכל	לא	Lekabel
32	רשו	הי	Veshiriah

5th Choir – Powers			
33	וחי	הי	Yeshavah
34	חהל	הי	Lehachah
35	קוכ	הי	Kevequiah
36	דנמ	לא	Mendiel

5th Choir – Powers			
37	ינא	לא	Eniel
38	מעח	הי	Chaamiah
39	עהר	לא	Rehaaiel
40	זיי	לא	Yeyeziel

6th Choir – Virtues			
41	ההה	לא	Hehihel
42	כימ	לא	Michael
43	לוו	הי	Vaveliah
44	הלי	הי	Yelahiah
45	לאס	הי	Saliyah
46	ירע	לא	Aaricl
47	לשע	הי	Aslayah
48	הימ	לא	Mihel

7th Choir – Principalities			
49	והו	לא	Dehooel
50	ינד	לא	Deneyel
51	שחה	הי	Hechachyah
52	ממע	הי	Aamemiah
53	אננ	לא	Nanael
54	תינ	לא	Nithael

7th Choir – Principalities			
55	הבמ	הי	Mibalaiah
56	יופ	הי	Payiel

8th Choir – Archangels			
57	ממנ	הי	Nehemiah
58	ליי	לא	Yeyalel
59	חרה	לא	Herachiel
60	רצמ	לא	Mitzreel
61	במו	לא	Vemibael
62	ההי	לא	Yahohel
63	ונע	לא	Aaneval
64	יחמ	לא	Mockael

9th Choir – Angels			
65	במד	הי	Demaiah
66	קנמ	לא	Menqel
67	עיא	לא	Ayael
68	ובח	הי	Chabeuyah
69	האר	לא	Rahael
70	מבי	הי	Yebomayah
71	ייה	לא	Hayeyel
72	מומ	הי	Mevimayah

These are the Shem ha-Mephorash or 72 Angels bearing the Name of God, grouped into 9 sets of eight each, corresponding to the 9 choirs of Angels, and also divided into four main groups of 18 each, with each group overseen by one of the four letters of The Name.

37

The Angels Zodiac Attributions

In astrology, a decan or ten degrees of a sign is called a *face*. This creates a total of 36 faces or decans. Additionally, each of these can be further divided, yielding 72 subdivisions of 5 degrees (quaternaries).

Each face or decan is governed by a planet, following the Sephardic order: Saturn, Jupiter, Mars, Sun, Venus, Mercury, and Moon.

The first three signs starting with Aries are governed by Yod (י), the letter of Fire. The water sign governs the second group of three signs. Cancer falls under the influence of Heh (ה), the letter of Water. The air sign leads the third group of three signs, with Libra under the influence of Vav (ו), the air letter. The last three signs, led by the earth sign Capricorn, are governed by Heh final (ה), the letter of Earth.

This system starts with Aries, representing the beginning of spring. Mathers and other sources begin with Leo, marking the start of summer.

It should be noted that the most powerful rule of Yod (י) is over the Fire Triplicity, Heh (ה) rules the Watery Triplicity, Vav (ו) governs the Airy Triplicity, and Heh (ה) presides over the Earth Triplicity.

	Sign	Decan	No. of Angel
	♈	♂	1 & 2
	♈	☉	3 & 4
	♈	♀	5 & 6
	♉	☿	7 & 8
	♉	☽	9 & 10
	♉	♄	11 & 12
	♊	♃	13 & 14
	♊	♂	15 & 16
	♊	☉	17 & 18
	♋	♀	19 & 20
	♋	☿	21 & 22
	♋	☽	23 & 24
	♌	♄	25 & 26
	♌	♃	27 & 28
	♌	♂	29 & 30
	♍	☉	31 & 32
	♍	♀	33 & 34
	♍	☿	35 & 36

	Sign	Decan	No. of Angel
ד	♎	☽	37 & 38
	♎	♄	39 & 40
	♎	♃	41 & 42
	♏	♂	43 & 44
	♏	☉	45 & 46
	♏	♀	47 & 48
	♐	☿	49 & 50
	♐	☽	51 & 52
	♐	♄	53 & 54
ה	♑	♃	55 & 56
	♑	♂	57 & 58
	♑	☉	59 & 60
	♒	♀	61 & 62
	♒	☿	63 & 64
	♒	☽	65 & 66
	♓	♄	67 & 68
	♓	♃	69 & 70
	♓	♂	71 & 72

Zeir Anpin – Lesser Countenance

In Kabbalah, Zeir Anpin is called the Lesser Countenance or Small Face. It refers to the six sephirot from Chesed to Yesod. Together, they form a divine face or personality. It symbolizes God's immanent divine presence in the world. The Small Face serves as a channel for divine light and blessings to flow into the lower realms and to humanity.

In the 22nd chapter of John's Apocalypse, it says:

> The Tree of Life, which bore twelve kinds of fruit and produced fruit every month, and the leaves of the Tree were for the healing of the nations. And there shall be no more curse: but the Throne of God and the Lamb shall be in it.

There are also other methods of creating sets of 72 Names from the verses. For example: (1) Writing them all right to left; (2) Permuting the letters using Temura. The meanings are then determined and shown below for the regular Shem Ha-Mephorash.

Note that all the letters of the Alphabet except Gimel (ג) are employed in the Shem Ha-Mephorash. Therefore, this letter, whose numerical value is three, is the Key to their construction.

The diagram below is from the 3 = 8 Altar. It depicts the Zodiac, the 12 tribes of the Sons of Jacob, and the 12 Apostles. The healing leaves are the Shem ha-Mephorash, or the divided name of the Zaur Anpin, The Microprosophus, The Christ, The Lamb of God, whose Throne is in the Tree, from which the Throne flows the River of the Waters of Life.

Zeir Anpin and the Shem ha-Mephorash.

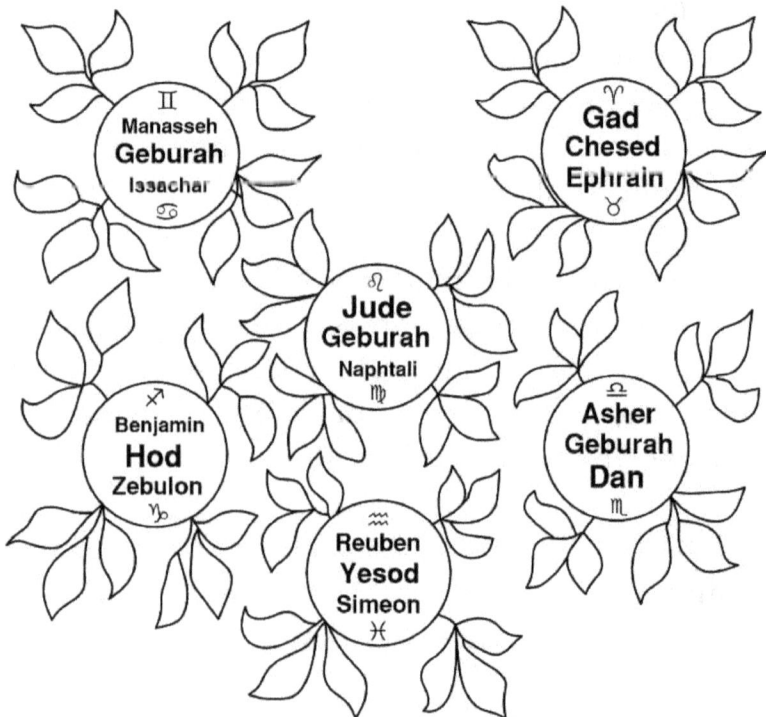

Shem and the 12 Zodiacal Hexagrams

The Number 72 = 6 x 12 or 12 Hexagrams, so that each Hexagram will represent by its angles the six quinaries of a sign that is written in the center. Thus, we have the formula of the 12 Talismans of the Shem Ha-Mephorash. For example:

Note that Leo Talisman above uses the first six Shem ha-Mephorash as the starting point, contrary to the Aries shown in the tables.

A suitable Psalm is composed in a circular pattern. The meanings of the 72 Names of God and the Angels of the Shem Ha-Mephorash are derived from these Psalms, each containing the Name IHVH, except for the 70th.

Bible Verses and the Shem ha-Mephorash

The earliest known source assigning specific Psalms of Invocation to each of the seventy-two angels is Thomas Rudd's manuscript preserved in the British Library. Its creation date is around 1640. The manuscript was later published as The Goetia of Dr. Rudd, Appendix 7.

Rudd's manuscripts appear to blend two traditions: the Shem ha-Mephorash angelic names from Exodus 14:19-21 and the Shimmush Tehillim (Use of the Psalms), forming a new ritual structure where each angel is associated with a specific psalm verse for invocation.

1. Vahaviah – God the Exalter
Psalm 3:4

2. Yelayel – Strength
Psalm 22:20

3. Saitel – Refuge, Fortress, and Confidence
Psalm 91:2

4. Olmiah – Concealed, Strong
Psalm 6:5

5. Mahashiah – Seeking Safety from Trouble
Psalm 34:5

6. Lelahel – Praiseworthy, declaring His works
Psalm 9:12

7. Akaiah – Long Suffering
Psalm 103:8

8. Kehethel – Adorable
Psalm 95:6

9. Hazayel – Merciful
Psalm 25:6

10. Aldiah – Profitable
Psalm 33:12

11. Laviah – To Be Exalted
Psalm 18:47

12. Hihaayah – Refuge
Psalm 10:1

13. Yezahel – Rejoicing Over All Things
Psalm 98:4

14. Mebahel – Guardian, Preserver
Psalm 9:10

15. Harayel – Aid
Psalm 44:22

16. Hoqmiah – Raise Up, Praying Day and Night
Psalm 88:2

17. Laviah – Wonderful
Psalm 8:2

18. Kelial – Worthy to be Invoked
Psalm 35:24

19. Livoyah – Hastening to Hear
Psalm 40:2

20. Phehilyah – Redeemer, Liberator
Psalm 120:2

21. Nelokhiel – Thou Alone
Psalm 31:15

22. Yeyayiel – Thy Right Hand
Psalm 121:5

23. Melohel – Turning Away Evil
Psalm 121:8

24. Chahaviah – Goodness in Himself
Psalm 33:18

25. Nithahiah – Wide in Extent, the Enlarger,
Wonderful
Psalm 9:2

26. Haayoh – Heaven in Secret
Psalm 119:145

27. Yirthiel – Deliverer
Psalm 140:2

28. Sahyoh – Taker Away of Evils
Psalm 71:17

29. Reyayel – Expectation
Psalm 54:6

30. Evamel – Patient
Psalm 71:5

31. Lekabel – Teacher, Instructor
Psalm 71:16

32. Veshiriah – Upright
Psalm 33:4

33. Yechavah – Knower of All Things
Psalm 94:11

34. Lehachiah – Clement, Merciful
Psalm 131:3

35. Keveqiah – To Be Rejoiced In
Psalm 71:1

36. Mendial – Honorable
Psalm 26:8

37. Aniel – Lord of Virtues
Psalm 80:4

38. Chaamiah – The Hope of All the Ends of the Earth
Psalm 91:9

39. Rehaaiel – Swift to Condone
Psalm 30:11

40. Yeyeziel – Making Joyful
Psalm 88:15

41. Hehihel – Triune
Psalm 120:2

42. Michael – Who Is Like Unto Him
Psalm 121:7

43. Vavaliah – King and Ruler
Psalm 88:13

44. Yelahiah – Abiding For Ever
Psalm 119:108

45. Saliah – Mover of All Things
Psalm 94:18

46. Aariel – Revealer
Psalm 145:9

47. Aaslayoh – Just Judge
Psalm 92:6

48. Mihal – Sending Forth as a Father
Psalm 98:2

49. Vehooel – Great and Lofty
Psalm 145:3

50. Deneyel – Merciful Judge
Psalm 145:8

51. Hechashyah – Secret and Impenetrable
Psalm 104:31

52. Aamamiah v Covered in Darkness
Psalm 7:17

53. Nanael – Caster Down of the Proud
Psalm 119:75

54. Nithael – Celestial King
Psalm 103:19

55. Mibahaiah – Eternal
Psalm 102:12

56. Pooyael – Supporting All Things
Psalm 145:14

57. Nemamiah – Lovable
Psalm 115:11

58. Yeveelel – Hearer of Cries
Psalm 6:3

59. Herochiel – Permeating All Things
Psalm 113:3

60. Mitzrael – Raising the Oppressed
Psalm 145:17

61. Vemibael – The Name Which is Over All
Psalm 118:2

62. Yahohel – The Supreme Ends, or Essence
Psalm 119:159

63. Aaneval – Rejoicing
Psalm 100:2

64. Machayel – Vivifying
Psalm 33:18

65. Damabayah – Fountain of Wisdom
Psalm 90:13

66. Menqel – Nourishing All
Psalm 38:21

67. Aayoel – Delights of the Sons of Men
Psalm 37:4

68. Chabooyah – Most Liberal Giver
Psalm 106:1

69. Rahael – Beholding All
Psalm 16:5

70. Yabomayah[1] – Produced by His Word
Psalm 1:1 [*Kabbalah of the Golden Dawn*, cites this
Biblical passage from Genesis 1:1]

71. Hahayel – Lord of the Universe
Psalm 108:30

72. Mevamayah – End of the Universe
Psalm 116:7

The 12 Ruling Archangels of the Signs

This table is from pages 86 & 305, *The Golden Dawn* by Israel Regardie, 6th Edition.

Ruling Archangels of the Signs			
Signs	יהוה Permutation	Name	Hebrew Name
♈	יהוה	Malchidael	מלכידאל
♉	יההו	Asmodel	אסמודאל
♊	יוהה	Ambriel	אמבריאל
♋	הוהי	Muriel	מוריאל
♌	הויה	Verchiel	ורכיאל
♍	ההוי	Hamaliel	המליאל
♎	והיה	Zuriel	זוריאל
♏	וההי	Barchiel	ברכיאל
♐	ויהה	Advachiel	אדוכיאל
♑	היהו	Hanael	הנאל
♒	היוה	Kambriel	כאמבריאל
♓	ההיו	Amnitziel	אמניציאל

The 12 Lesser Assistant Angels of the Signs

This table is from page 86 & 305 *The Golden Dawn* by Israel Regardie, 6th Edition.

Lesser Assistant Angels of the Signs		
Signs	Name	Hebrew
♈	Sharhiel	שרהיאל
♉	Araziel	ארזיאל
♊	Saraiel	סראיאל
♋	Pakiel	פכיאל
♌	Sharatiel	שרטיאל
♍	Schaltiel (Shelathiel)	שלתיאל
♎	Chedeqiel	חדקיאל
♏	Saitziel	סאיציאל
♐	Saritiel	סמקיאל
♑	Sameqiel	סריטיאל
♒	Tsakmakiel	צכמקיאל
♓	Vakabiel	וכביאל

The 12 Angels Ruling the 12 Heavenly Houses and their Signs

The Angels Ruling the Heavenly Houses			
House	Signs	Name	Hebrew
Ascendant	♈	Ayel	איאל
2nd	♉	Tual (Toel)	טואל
3rd	♊	Giel	גיאל
4th	♋	Kaael (Kael)	כאאל
5th	♌	Ovel	עואל
6th	♍	Viel (Veyel)	וייאל
7th	♎	Yahel	יהאל
8th	♏	Susol	סוסול
9th	♐	Suiosel	סויעסאל
10th	♑	Kasniyoyah (Kashenyayah)	כשניעיה
11th	♒	Ansoel (Ansuel)	אנסואל
12th	♓	Pashiel	פשיאל

52

The Zodiacal Signs in Hebrew

Hebrew Zodiacal Signs		
Signs	Name	Hebrew
♈	Telah (Teleh)	טלה
♉	Sor (Shor)	שור
♊	Teomim	תאומים
♋	Sarton	סרטן
♌	Aryeh (Ari)	אריה
♍	Betulah	בתולה
♎	Maznaim	מאזנים
♏	Oqreb (Akrab)	עקרב
♐	Qesheth	קשת
♑	Gadi (Gedi)	גדי
♒	Dali (Deli)	דלי
♓	Dogim (Dagim)	דגים

Lord of Triplicity by Day

This table is from *777*, page 26, table 144.

Lord of Triplicity by Day			
Signs	Name	Hebrew	Godwin
♈	Sataraaton (Seteraton)	סטרעטן	
♉	Raydal (Raydel)	ראידאל	
♊	Saadesch (Sarash)	סעדש	סערש
♋	Raadar	רעדר	
♌	Sagham (Sanahem)	סנהם	סנהם
♍	Laslara	לסלרא	
♎	Targabon (Thergebon)	תרגבון	
♏	Bethchon	ביתחון	
♐	Almoz (Ahoz)	אהנז	אהוז
♑	Sagdoloi (Sandali)	סגדלעי	סנדלעי
♒	Osur (Athor)	עתור	
♓	Ramara	רמרא	

Lord of Triplicity by Night

This table is from 777, page 29, table 145. English transliterations of Hebrew listed in parentheses are from Godwin's Cabalistic Encyclopedia.

Lord of Triplicity by Night		
Signs	Name	Hebrew
♈	Spotaoy (Sapatavi)	ספעטאוי
♉	Totes (Totath)	טוטת
♊	Ogeromaan (Ogarman)	עוגרמען
♋	Ochal (Akel)	עכאל
♌	Zilbrachis (Zalbarhith)	זלברהית
♍	Sosia (Sasia)	ססיא
♎	Achodraen (Achadraon)	אחודראון
♏	Sahqnov	סהקנב
♐	Labramaim	לברמים
♑	Elvir (Aloyar)	אלויר
♒	Palaon (Polayan)	פלאון
♓	Nisdorigal[1]	נתדוריגאל

[1] Godwin spelling: Nathdorinel (נתדורנאל)

Tetragrammaton and Shem

The following note further illustrates the connection between YHVH and the Shem ha-Mephorash.

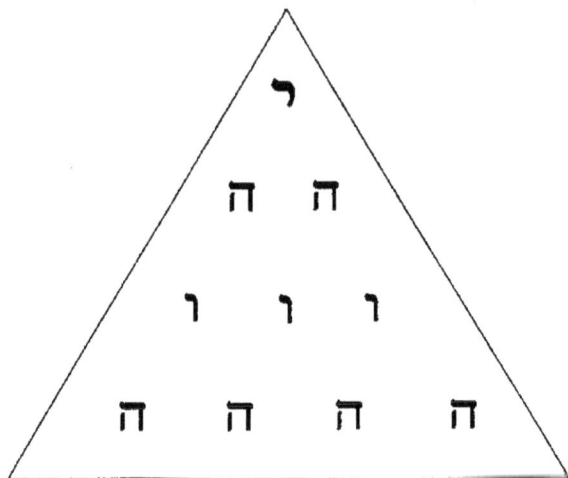

Write the Tetragrammaton with the apex pointing upward. Its component letters form a triangle by extending each downward stroke beyond the space of the line above. At the top is a single line; below that, two Hehs; then three Vaus; and finally four Hehs. This arrangement creates a triangle of ten letters representing the Ten Sephiroth: the topmost Yod corresponds to Kether, the two Hehs to Chokmah and Binah, the three Vaus to Chesed, Geburah, and Tiphareth, and the four final Hehs to Netzach, Hod, Yesod, and Malkuth.

Then flip the triangle and arrange it in descending order: four Yods, three Hehs, two Vaus, and one final Heh. The total adds up to 72, which is the number of Schem ha-Mephoresh.

If we invert the Triangle and list it in descending order: four Yods, three Hehs, two Vaus, and one final Heh, we will find that the total number is 72, the same as that of the Scheme ha-Mephoresch.

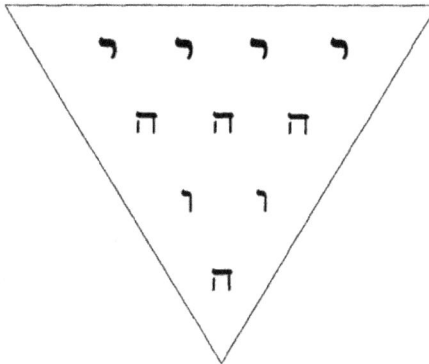

י י י י

ה ה ה

ו ו

ה

# Letters	Letter	Value
4	Yod י	40 = 4 x 10
3	Heh ה	15 = 3 x 5
2	Vav ו	12 = 2 x 6
1	Heh ה	5 = 5 x 1

But the best of the forms is written Yod, Heh, etc. Thus:

Yod is 10 and equals Atziluth.

Yod-Heh is 15 and equals Briah.

Yod-Heh-Vau is 21 and equals Yetzirah.

Yod-Heh-Vau-Heh is 26 and equals Assiah.

Ahaya (אהיה) equals 21. Therefore, *Ahaya* and *Yetzirah* are equivalent. Similarly, *IHVH* and *Assiah* are also equivalent. Additionally, 15 is Yah (יה), the divine name of Chokmah and the 8th Sephira Hod. Yod (10) is the original letter and a symbol of flame and emanation (Atziluth). Interestingly, the numbers assigned to the four worlds in this system add up to 72: 10 + 15 + 21 + 26.

Chapter 2 Notes

Although Shem ha.mephorash is Hebrew in origin, the addition of angelic endings (el and yah) to the names is not. Johann Reuchlin (1455-1522) added these suffixes. Later, Dr. Rudd's manuscripts include the association with the Psalms.

In Jewish sources like Sefer Raziel ha-Malakh or Sefer ha-Zohar, the 72 names are regarded as divine attributes or powers, not individual angels. They appear without suffixes and without psalm correspondences.

CHAPTER 3 – Chaldean Oracles

Excerpts from the
Chaldean Oracles of Zoroaster

Introduction

The Chaldean Oracles are some of the most mysterious and influential texts from late antiquity. They are credited to Zoroaster; however, this might refer to a school of thought rather than a specific individual.

The surviving fragments of the Chaldean Oracles of Zoroaster date to the late 2nd century AD and were compiled by Julian the Theurgist and his son from other philosophers' writings.

The text is a cornerstone of theurgy. In ritual, the ultimate goal is uniting the soul with the divine. This is achieved through symbolic ascent, as described in the path workings of this order and our ascent up the Tree of Life.

The Chaldean Oracles cosmology outlines a radiant hierarchy descending from the First Father through the Paternal Mind and Hecate, into the luminous fire-bearing souls that uphold the worlds. If you're unfamiliar with the Chaldean Oracles, read the end of chapter notes first to familiarize yourself with the cosmology.

The universal ideas expressed in the Oracles served as a bridge between Platonism, Hermeticism, and Kabbalah. Therefore, it is one of the intellectual roots of the Western esoteric tradition.

SECTION 1

Theurgists assert that He is a God and celebrate Him as both older and younger, as a circulating and eternal God, as understanding the whole number of all things moving in the World, and infinite through His power and energizing a spiral force.

The God of the Universe, eternal, limitless, both young and old, possesses a spiral force.

For the Eternal Aeon – according to the Oracle – is the cause of never-failing life, of unwearied power and unsluggish energy.

Thus, the mysterious God is called silent by the divine beings and is said to agree with the Mind and to be known to human souls through the power of the Mind alone.

The Chaldeans refer to the God Dionysos (or Bacchus) as Iao in the Phoenician language (instead of the Intelligible Light), and he is also called Sabaoth, indicating that He is above the Seven poles, that is, the Demiurgos.

For nothing imperfect emanates from the Paternal Principle.

The Father did not instill fear, but He infused persuasion.

The Father has apprehended Himself and has not limited His Fire to His intellectual power.

Such is the mind, energized before energy, while it had not gone forth, but remained in the Paternal Depth, and the Adytum of God nourished silence.

All things came from that one Fire. The Father created everything and handed it over to the Second Mind, whom all nations of men call the First.

The Second Mind controls the Empyrean World.

What the intelligible says; it communicates through understanding.

Power resides with them, but the Mind comes from Him. The Father's Mind moves upon the subtle Guiders, which shimmer with unyielding and relentless fire tracings.

...After the Paternal Conception, the Soul resides, a heat that animates everything.

...For He placed the Intelligible in the Soul, and the Soul in a dull body. Even so, the Father of Gods and Men placed them within us.

Natural works coexist with the intellectual illumination of the Father. For it is the Soul that decorated the vast Heaven and continues to beautify it after the Father, but Her dominion is established above.

The Soul, being a brilliant Fire, by the power of the Father, remains immortal, is Mistress of Life, and fills up the many recesses of the bosom of the World. With channels being mixed, she performs the works of incorruptible Fire.

Not in Matter did the First Fire beyond enclose His active Power, but in Mind; for the one who shapes the Fiery World is the Mind of Mind.

Who first emerged from the Mind, wrapping one Fire in the other Fire, binding them together so He could mingle the fountain craters while keeping the brilliance of His Fire pure.

And from there, a fiery whirlwind draws down the brilliance of the flashing flame, penetrating the abysses of the Universe; from that point downward, their wondrous rays extend.

The Monad originally existed; and the Paternal Monad still subsists.

When the Monad is extended, the Dyad is generated.

And beside Him is seated the Dyad, which gleams with intellectual sections, to govern everything and organize all that is unordered.

The Mind of the Father said that all things should be cut into Three, whose Will assented, and immediately all things were divided.

The Mind of the Eternal Father said into Three, governing all things by Mind. The Father mingled every Spirit from this Triad. All things are supplied from the bosom of this Triad. All things are governed and exist in this Triad, for all things bow before the Three Supernals.

From then flows the Form of the Triad, being pre-existing; not the First Essence, but that through which all things are measured. And Virtue, Wisdom, and multiversal Truth appeared within it. For in each World, the Triad shines, over which the Monad rules.

The First Course is Sacred; the Sun is in the middle, and the Earth is heated from within.

Exalted above and energizing Light, Fire, Ether, and Worlds.

SECTION 2

The Mind of the Father erupted in a resonant roar, grasping omniform Ideas through invincible Will; these Ideas, emanating from a single source, flow forth because from the Father, both Will and End, are connected with Him through alternating life and varying vehicles. However, they were separated by Intellectual Fire and distributed among other Intellectuals. For the King of all, previously placed before the polymorphous World, is a Type—an intellectual, incorruptible form, whose imprint is sent throughout the World. This imprint causes the Universe to shine with diverse Ideas, all originating from a single foundation—One and only. From this foundation, the others emerge, spread and separated across the Universe's various bodies, swirling in swarms through its vast depths, continuously radiating outward in endless streams.

They are intellectual concepts from the Paternal
Fountain, sharing generously in the brilliance of Fire
at the peak of unresting Time.

But the primary self-perfect Fountain of the Father poured forth these primordial Ideas. These, being many, descend swiftly upon the shining Worlds, and within them are contained the Three Supernals. They serve as the guardians of the works of the Father and the One Mind, the Intelligible.

All things exist together in the Intelligible World.

But all Intellect understands the Deity, for Intellect exists not without the Intelligible, neither apart from Intellect does the Intelligible subsist. Intellect exists not without the Intelligible; apart from it, it subsists not.

By the Intellect, He contains the Intelligibles and introduces the Soul into the Worlds. By the Intellect, He contains the Intelligibles and introduces Sense into the Worlds.

This Paternal Intellect understands the intelligibles, adorns ineffable things, and has sown symbols throughout the world.

This order marks the beginning of all sections.

The Intelligible is the principle of all sections. The Intelligible is like food for those who understand.

The oracles concerning the Orders before the Heavens as ineffable, and they add -- It hath Mystic Silence.

Because it is the Operator, it is the Giver of Life Bearing Fire, as it fills the life-giving bosom of Hecate and infuses the Synoches with the energizing power of Fire, endured with mighty strength.

He gave His Whirlwinds to guard the Supernals, blending the proper force of His strength into the Synoches. But likewise, as many as serve the material Synoches.

Rhea, the Fountain and River of the Blessed Intellectuals, having first received the powers of all things in Her Ineffable Bosom, continuously pours forth creation upon all things.

He is a luminescent force, shining with Intellectual Sections. He shined with Intellectual Sections and filled everything with love.

To the intellectual whirl of intellectual fire, all things are subordinate through the persuasive guidance of the Father.

0! How Inflexible Intellectual Rulers Have Shaped the World.

From Him come the Amilicti [a triad of pure, unpolluted divine beings], the all-relentless thunders, and the whirlwind receiving Bosoms of the all-splendid Strength of Hecate, father-begotten; and He who encircles the brilliance of Fire; and the Strong Spirit of the Poles, all fiery beyond.

Another fountain that leads to the Empyrean World [the highest heaven] is the Fountain of Fountains, which symbolizes the boundary of all fountains. All fountains and principles swirl around and are constantly in ceaseless motion.

Father begotten Light, which alone has drawn from the strength of the Father the Flower of the mind, and has the power to understand the Paternal mind. It instills into all Fountains and Principles the power of understanding and the function of ceaseless revolution.

Typhon, Echidna, and Python, as children of Tartaros and Gaia, who was shaped by Uranos, together form a sort of Chaldean Triad—a guardian and inspector of all chaotic creations.

Certain irrational demons (mindless elementals) derive their subsistence from the aerial rulers, so the oracle says, being the charioteer of the aerial, terrestrial, and aquatic dogs.

The Aquatic, when referring to Divine Natures, indicates a government intrinsically linked to water; therefore, the Oracle calls the Aquatic Gods Waterwalkers.

There are certain Water Elementals that Orpheus calls Nereides, living in the higher exhalations of Water, such as appear in damp, cloudy Air, whose bodies are sometimes seen (as Zoroaster taught) by sharper eyes, especially in Persia and Africa.

SECTION 3

The Father conceived ideas, and he animated all mortal bodies. For the Father of Gods and men placed the Mind (nous) in the Soul (psyche) and placed them in the (human) body.

The Paternal Mind has planted symbols in the Soul.

Having blended the Vital Spark from two distinct sources, Mind and Divine Spirit, and adding a third, Holy Love, the venerable Charioteer unites all things. Filling the Soul with deep Love.

The soul of man, in a way, embraces God. Having nothing mortal, she is completely intoxicated with God. For she takes pride in the harmony that sustains the mortal body.

The more powerful Souls perceive Truth through themselves and are of a more inventive Nature. Such Souls are saved through their strength, according to the Oracle.

The girders of the Soul, which sustain her breathing, are easily loosened.

When you see a soul set free, the Father sends another so that the number may be complete.

Understanding the works of the Father, they avoid the shameless Wing of Fate; they are placed in God, drawing forth strong light-bearers, descending from the Father, from whom, as they descend, the Soul gathers the empyrean fruits, the soul-nourishing flower.

This Animastic Spirit, which blessed men have called the Pneumatic Soul, becomes a god, an all-various Demon, and an Image (disembodied), and in this form of Soul, suffers her punishments. The Oracles, too, agree with this account, for they compare the Soul's activity in Hades to the misleading visions of a dream.

One life after another, originating from widely spread sources. Passing from above to the opposite side, through the Earth's Center, and reaching the fiery middle center, where the life-giving fire extends down to the material world.

Water is a symbol of life; therefore, Plato and the gods before him refer to it as (the Soul). Sometimes, it represents all living water, and other times, it is seen as a particular fountain of it.

O man, of daring nature, you subtle creation.

Since the soul constantly experiences various events over a certain period, it is now compelled to revisit everything and replicate a similar pattern of creation in the world, according to Zoroaster, who believes that when the same causes recur, the same effects will inevitably follow.

According to Zoroaster, the ethereal vestment of the soul always revolves (reincarnates) within us.

The Oracles delivered by the Gods celebrate the essential source of every Soul: the Empyrean, the Ethereal, and the Material. This source they separate from (Zoogonothea), the vivifying Goddess (Rhea), from whom (suspending the entire Fate) they create two series or levels; one is animistic, or belonging to the Soul, and the other belongs to Fate. They claim that the Soul comes from the animistic series but sometimes becomes subordinate to Fate; when it enters an irrational state of being, it becomes subject to Fate rather than to Providence.

SECTION 4

The Matrix encompasses all things, entirely divisible but inseparable. From it, many generations of various Matter arise. These create atoms, visible forms, physical bodies, and objects designed for matter.

The Nymphs of the Fountains, all Water Spirits, and terrestrial, aerial, and astral forms are the Lunar Riders and Rulers of all Matter, the Celestial, the Starry, and what lies in the Abysses.

The Gods claim that Matter permeates the entire universe.

All Divine Natures are incorporeal, but bodies arc attached to them for your benefit. Bodies cannot contain incorporeals because of the Corporeal Nature in which they are concentrated.

For the Paternal Self-begotten Mind, understanding His works, planted in all the fiery bonds of love, causes all things to continue loving for an infinite time. The connected series of things might remain intellectually in the Light of the Father; the elements of the World could keep their course in mutual attraction.

The Maker of all things, self-operating, created the World. There was also a certain Mass of Fire: all these things Self-Operating He produced, so that the Body of the Universe might be shaped, that the World might be revealed, and not appear membranous.

He absorbed the images into himself, surrounding his form with them. For they are an imitation of his Mind, but what is created has some of the qualities of the Body.

The Oracles state that the types of Characters and other Divine visions manifest in the Ether (or Astral Light). In this, things without figures are given figures.

He creates the World of Fire, Air, Water, Earth, and the all-nourishing Ether. Placing Earth in the middle, with Water below the Earth and Air above both.

He fixed many wandering stars not through hard, painful effort, but with steady, unmoving resolve, pushing fire into fire.

He formed a septenary of wandering existences (the planetary globes), stabilizing their disorder in well-disposed zones.

He made them six in number, and for the seventh, He cast into the fiery sun's midst.

The Vast Sun and the Brilliant Moon. As rays of light, his locks flow outward, ending in sharp points.

And of the Solar Circles, the Lunar, clashings, and the Aerial Recesses; the Melody of Ether, the Sun, the Moon, and the Air phases.

The most mystical of teachings tells us that His wholeness exists in the Supra-mundane Orders, where a Solar World and Boundless Light thrive, as the Oracles of the Chaldeans affirm.

According to the Oracles, the Sun more accurately measures everything through time, being itself the time of time.

The Sun is a Fire, a channel of Fire, and a dispenser of Fire.

The Ethereal Course, the vast movement of the Moon, and the Aerial fluxes. 0 Ether, Sun, and Spirit of the Moon, you are the chiefs of the Air.

The Goddess brings forth the Vast Sun and the luminous Moon. She gathers them, receiving the Melody of Ether, the Sun, the Moon, and everything contained in the Air.

Unwearied Nature rules over the worlds and works, so that the heavens drawing downward might run an eternal course, and the other periods of the Sun, Moon, Seasons, Night, and Day might be accomplished. And above the shoulders of that great goddess is Nature in her vastness exalted.

Zoroaster calls the similarities of material forms to the ideals of the Soul of the World – Divine Allurements.

Do not direct your mind toward the vast surfaces of the Earth, for the Plant of Truth does not grow on the ground. Nor measure the Sun's motions, gathering rules, for it is carried by the Eternal Will of the Father, not solely for your sake. Dismiss from your mind the impetuous course of the Moon, for she moves always by necessity. The stars' progression was not created for you. The wide flight of birds offers no real knowledge, nor does the dissection of victims' entrails; they are all mere tricks used for greed. Flee from these if you wish to enter the sacred paradise of piety, where Virtue, Wisdom, and Equity are gathered.

Stoop not down unto the Darkly-Splendid World, wherein continually lies a faithless Depth, and Hades wrapped in clouds, delighting in unintelligible images, precipitous, winding, a black ever-rolling Abyss; ever espousing a Body unluminous, formless and void.

Don't stoop down, for a precipice lies beneath the Earth, reached by a descending ladder with seven steps, and an evil and deadly force's throne is established.

Don't stay on the edge with worthless matter, for there is a place for your image in a glorious realm.

Do not invoke the visible image of Nature's soul.

Defile not the Spirit, nor deepen a superficial surface. Enlarge not your Destiny. Change not the barbarous Names of Evocation, for there are sacred Names in every language given by God, holding in the Sacred Rites an Ineffable Power.

Do not go out when the Lictor (court official) passes by.

Let fiery hope nourish you on the Angelic plane.

The Gods urge us to understand the radiant form of Light. It is your duty to move toward the Light and the Rays of the Father, from whom a Soul (Psyche) was sent to you, endowed with much mind (Nous).

Learn the Intelligible, for it subsists beyond the Mind. There is a certain Intelligible One whom you can understand with the Flower of Mind.

However, the Paternal Mind does not accept the soul's aspiration until she has emerged from her oblivious state and speaks the Word, restoring the Memory of the pure paternal Symbol.

Things divine are not reachable by mortals who only understand the body but only by those stripped of their garments and who reach the summit.

Having armed the full power of shining Light, with triple strength to strengthen the Soul and the Mind, He must focus the Mind on the various Symbols and avoid wandering aimlessly on the empyrean path, but with concentration.

Explore the River of the Soul, whence, or in what order you have come: although you may become a servant to the body, you may again rise to the Order from which you descended, joining works to sacred reason.

Every path toward the liberated Soul spreads the rays of Fire. Let the eternal depth of your Soul guide you, but sincerely lift your eyes upward.

Man, being an intelligent mortal, must restrain his soul so that she does not suffer terrestrial misfortune but is saved.

If you extend the Fiery Mind to the work of righteousness, you will preserve the flexible body.

According to the Oracle, we should escape the crowd of men moving in a herd.

Who knows himself knows everything within himself.

But these are mysteries which I evolve in the profound Abyss of the Mind.

Theurgists are not to be considered part of the herd subjected to Fate.

The Furies are the Enforcers of Men.

A similar fire flashingly extends through the rushing air, a formless fire from which emerges the image of a voice or an even more abundant flashing light, revolving and whirling out, crying aloud. There is also a vision of the fire-flashing courser of light, or a child borne aloft on the shoulders of a celestial steed, fiery, clothed with gold, naked, or shooting shafts of light with a bow, standing on the steed's shoulders. If your meditation continues, you will unite all these symbols into the form of a lion.

When you behold that holy and formless Fire shining brightly through the depths of the Universe: Hear you the Voice of Fire.

ORACLES FROM PORPHYRY

Above the Celestial Lights burns an Incorruptible Flame that is always shining: the Spring of Life, the Source of all Beings, the Origin of everything! This Flame creates all things, and nothing perishes except what it consumes. It reveals itself by itself. This Fire cannot be contained anywhere. It has no Body or Matter. It encompasses the Heavens. From it, small Sparks emerge, fueling the Fires of the Sun, the Moon, and the Stars. Behold! This is what I know of God! Do not seek to understand more about Him, for that is beyond your ability, no matter how wise you are. As for everything else, know that unjust and wicked Man cannot hide himself from the Presence of God!

No subtlety or excuse can hide anything from His piercing Eyes. Everything is full of God, and God is in everything!

There is in God an immense profundity of flame! Nevertheless, the heart should not fear approaching this adorable fire or being touched by it; it will never be consumed by this sweet fire, whose mild and tranquil heat makes the binding, the harmony, and the duration of the world: nothing persists but this fire, which is God Himself. No person begat Him; He is without mother; He knows everything and can be taught nothing.

He is infallible in His designs, and His name is unspeakable. Behold now what God is! As for us, we are His messengers. We are but a small part of God.

Chapter 3 Notes

The Chaldean Oracles do not speak in the language of philosophy but in revelation — fragments of vision expressed through hieratic symbols. To understand them, one must see their structure as a living fire-based cosmology.

This radiant chain descends from the ineffable First Father, through the Paternal Mind and Hecate, into the fire-bearing souls that sustain the worlds. It reflects a pattern of emanation seen in the four worlds of Kabbalah, Atziluth, Briah, Yetzirah, and Assiah, and acts as a bridge among Platonism, Hermeticism, and Kabbalah. From this synthesis, the very foundation of the Western esoteric tradition emerged.

(Adapted from cosmological analysis by ChatGPT, 2025.)

1. The Radiant Chain of Emanation

The Chaldean Oracles depict reality as a radiant hierarchy — a continuous chain of light descending from the ineffable First Father (the One Beyond Being). This source is completely transcendent, "beyond intellect and essence," yet it overflows with luminous power. The act of emanation is not creation ex nihilo but a spread of divine fire — a flowing outpouring of intelligible light that remains connected to its source.

From this primal unity proceeds the *Paternal Mind,* the first manifestation of divine consciousness. The Father and the Mind are not separate beings but two aspects of the same mystery: the Father as hidden root, and the Mind as the first expression or mirror of that hiddenness. The Mind is called "the intellect of the Father" — both origin and boundary of all subsequent existence.

2. The Role of Hecate as Mediatrix

Between the Paternal Mind and the manifested cosmos stands *Hecate*, the luminous mediatrix. She is not the lunar goddess of later magic, but a vast metaphysical principle — the boundary (*horos*) between the intelligible and the manifest. The Oracles call her the "membrane" or "veil" between the unbegotten fire and the created worlds. Through her, the divine light is refracted and distributed into multiplicity without rupture.

Hecate's *womb of fire* is the space of creation; she contains the "flower of fire" that transmits the creative energies from the Father's Mind into the "fire-bearing intellects," the divine souls that shape and govern the cosmos. Therefore, she embodies both preservation and transmission: the guardian of the Father's ineffable light and the channel through which the divine is revealed.

3. The Fire-Bearing Souls and the Cosmos

Below Hecate, the luminous or fire-bearing souls, those who sustain the worlds, are revealed. These are the cosmic intermediaries who transform divine order into physical form. Every world, from the celestial spheres to the sublunary realm, is animated by such souls. They are sparks of the paternal fire, reflecting the eternal order into time and space.

The descent of these souls signifies the creation of the cosmic hierarchy: the Empyrean (realm of pure fire), the Ethereal (starry heavens), and the Material (the visible world). Yet even at the lowest level, the world remains filled with divine radiance. The human soul shares this fire, and through theurgic ascent, by "rekindling the spark within," it can trace the chain back to the Father.

4. Summary Insight

In short, the Chaldean cosmology envisions a radiant procession:

The First Father > Paternal Mind > Hecate > Fire-bearing Souls > Cosmos

Each level mirrors the one above it with diminishing light intensity. The entire system is both metaphysical and mystical: a map showing how divine light flows outward to create, and how the soul may ascend back by reversing that flow — returning from multiplicity to unity.

CHAPTER 4 – Flaming Cube Ritual

By Paul Clark
And Frater L. F.

In the first chapter of the Book of Formation (Sepher Yetzirah), we see an image of the Creator sealing the six directions of space, thereby establishing the Cosmic Cube. Note that the Creator is depicted at the center of the Cube, in the "Palace of Holiness." Since this Cube has no fixed size, its center point can (and does) exist anywhere. Compare this to the description of Kether as "a circle whose circumference is nowhere and center is everywhere." Thus, God exists at all or any possible points within you!

The following ritual can be used to clear a space for meditation. It can also be used alongside the meditations on the Chaldean Oracles that are performed at this level. Moreover, it aligns the operator with the energy currents of the Universe. Additionally, during the ritual, the operator identifies with the Deity; it functions as a form of self-consecration or an exercise in personal spiritual growth.

This ritual should be performed once a week, preferably on the same night each week, by the Philosophus until the date of the Portal Initiation. A careful record of this should be maintained in the magical journal and presented to the Chief during the examination. A demonstration of Version One is required as part of the examination for this grade.

The Ritual (Version One)

In the following, you will form the six sides of the Cube around yourself, each wall a different color. Since each side is nine feet square and you sit at the center, the Eastern wall will be four and a half feet in front of you, the Western wall four and a half feet behind you, and the Southern and Northern walls four and a half feet to your right and left, respectively.

It might be helpful to sketch the basic outline of the Cube without any color before you start. It can also help your visualization to imagine yourself floating in vast, dark space as if you were the Creator before the first Word was spoken. These aids are unique to each person and are not really part of the ritual.

Flaming Cube Meditation

The operator is sitting in a room facing east.

Visualize yourself as a point of primal light, shimmering, pulsating, glowing with life. Say aloud:

In the beginning, the Creator existed, solitary, at the center of space, one and one alone.

Height

Observe a ray of this light stretch toward the ceiling, spreading into a 9-foot square of yellow light. Say:

He sealed the Height, turned Above and sealed it with *(intone)* **Yod-Heh-Vav.**   (Notes: F, C, C#)

Depth

Now, see a ray project onto the floor, expanding into a nine-foot-square of *blue* light. Say:

He sealed the Depth, turned below, and sealed it with (*intone*) **Vav-Heh-Yod**. (C#, C, F)

East

See a ray of light projected to the East, expanding into a 9-foot square *green* wall, and say:

He sealed the East, turned forward, and sealed it with **Heh-Yod-Vav**. (C, F, C#)

West

Project a ray to the West and see it expand as before into a 9-foot square of *violet* light. Then say:

He sealed the West, turned backward, and sealed it with **Vav-Yod-Heh**. (C#, F, C)

North

See a ray of light projecting to your left where it becomes a square of *red* light, and say:

He sealed the North, turned to the left, and sealed it with **Heh-Vav-Yod**. (C, C#, F)

South

To complete the Cube, see a ray project to the right expand into an *orange* square, and say:

"He sealed the South, turned to the right, and sealed it with (*intone*) **Yod-Vav-Heh.**" (F, C#, C)

Qabalistic Cross

The Cube should now be visualized as fully formed. After any other meditation, conclude with the Qabalistic Cross.

This might seem like a dull, mechanical use of your imagination. In reality, it's quite the opposite. Even moderate success will give you a sense of power in motion, as no language can truly express. Remember, the main goal is to feel yourself projecting this imaginary Cube of Space from the very core of your being.

Version Two

Once Version One is mastered, the Philosophus can learn and practice the following variation of the Ritual of the Flaming Cube. This second version is supplementary, and there will be no test. The ritual is essentially the same as version one with two specific differences: (1) the visualizations are different and more detailed, (2) the energies are perceived as flowing from the sides of the Cube inward, toward the operator. This may also serve as a powerful preliminary, especially for meditation.

Stand facing east.

(1) Visualize directly above you a 9-foot square of yellow, in the center of which is a Caduceus with double-twined serpents of red and blue, and the entire wand alive, glowing with orange-gold fire. Draw a beam of light from this center downward through you vertically. Intone Yod-Heh-Vav.

(2) Visualize a silver Cup directly beneath you on a 9-foot square of blue, shallow enough to appear as a crescent. This Cup receives light from above and, blending into its essence, reflects a pure, calm light upward. Complete the union of these two opposites within yourself, at the heart center, as you intone: Vav-Heh-Yod.

(3) In the East, visualize a 9-foot square of green with an Ankh of glowing red flame. Feel this primal Life-Force flowing from the symbol toward you, passing through your heart center. Intone Heh-Yod-Vav.

(4) Experience yourself as a lens for this beam of the Life-Force. Let it pass through you to illuminate a grand spinning Wheel behind you, set against a violet backdrop. The Wheel circulates the received life current and returns it as a beam that intersects the other three at your heart center. Intone Vav-Yod-Heh.

(5) To your right [South], imagine a 9-foot orange square with the magnificent, flaming face of the Sun at its center, shining in its most glorious splendor. Admire this solar image as your intuition guides you. From it, a ray of light emerges and intersects with others at a point near your heart. Intone Yod-Vav-Heh.

(6) To your left [North], visualize a tall tower reaching heavenward in the Place of Greatest Darkness against the night sky. Identify with this upright tower. Let the beam of sunlight pass through you to contact the image of this tower. Feel it receive the energies transmitted from the Sun. As you recite the Name Heh-Vav-Yod, feel the lightning flash forth and experience the brief, endless Silence that follows.

(7) Focus your awareness on where the six rays of light meet within you. See there, a black pearl, dark as the imagination allows, yet lustrous and gleaming. As the six rays converge and flow into this sphere, let your attention move into it.

It may be that you discover an infinite depth to explore, or that this ebony sphere is, in fact, a sphere of all light, or even that as you move into its profound depths, you realize that you are paradoxically moving outward through infinite and absorbing Space. Whatever presents itself to you, let this be the gateway to your meditation period, and by intoning the name, Elohim, let yourself enter the SILENCE, which is the Palace of Holiness at the center of ALL.

CHAPTER 5 – The A-n's Role

By Soror F.

A Philosophus is qualified to serve as A-n for six months. In a fully operational Lodge, this is the fifth officer role (floor position) where each member serves; A-n needs to have at least the grade of 4 = 7 of Philosophus.

DUTIES OF THE A-n

Presiding over the twilight and darkness that surrounds us in the absence of the sun of life and light, the A-n guards the Gate of the West. He/she also assists in the reception of the Candidate and supervises subordinate officers in the execution of their duties.

Before each convocation, the A-n needs to do the following preparation work: Draw an invoking Earth Pentagram over the top of his or her sword in shimmering blue light using the index finger. Hold the sword between the palms and feel a current of pure Light flowing into it through the palms. Image the sword glowing with living, loving blue etheric Light.

The Archangel Sandalphon

In Hebrew and Christian symbolism, A-n is the great archangel Sandalphon. She is the Preparer of the Path.

The basic image of Sandalphon is that of a noble angelic figure, full of grace and winged, with dark curly brown hair and dressed in Earth tones such as citrine, russet, deep indigo, and olive green. The highlights on the robe, its shadows, and contours are white, creating a flashing effect. Sandalphon holds a sword in his right hand. A helpful tip is to imagine yourself as Sandalphon within a radiant dark indigo sphere that matches your height. Once this sphere of light is visualized in your mind, it usually becomes the easiest image to recall during the ritual.

The Sword

The A-n's ensign of office is the sword, symbolizing severity and judgment. The sword represents the forces of the pillar of Severity as a whole, but the locations of the Sephiroth are not necessarily indicated on it. The guard is Hod and is usually made of brass; the grip is the path of Shin and may be scarlet, and the pommel, Malkuth, might be black. The grip used to wield it, being the path of Shin, represents the universe governed by the flaming force of Severity and signifies the A-n wielding the forces of Divine Severity. The blade demonstrates this concept from Hod to Binah, covering Geburah through the paths of Mem and Cheth.

Remember that the divine name of Malkuth is Adonai (אדני): its number is 65, which is 5 times 13. Five represents Geburah, and 13 represents *Achad* (אחד), meaning love. These two principles govern Malkuth.

The Lamen

The lamen of the A-n is a triangle with three Tau Crosses in the center. The white triangle symbolizes the three paths connecting Malkuth to the other Sephiroth. The Tau Cross represents the hilt of the uplifted sword, which is the emblem of the A-n. As a symbol of salvation, the Tau Cross also signifies salvation from death and eternal life. The Hebrew value of Tau is 400, and the total value of the three Tau Crosses is 1200. Therefore, the three Tau Crosses relate to *Hua* (הוא).

which has a Hebrew value of 12, and *Hua* is the vengeful angel. It is, therefore, a fitting symbol on the lamen of the A-n, since the A-n also symbolizes the Avenger of the Gods.

The black field symbolizes darkness and ignorance, representing the grave of error. The white triangle, set within the surrounding darkness, is itself circumscribed by the Circle of Light. Additionally, the lamen signifies "The Light that shineth in darkness though the darkness comprehendeth it not." It affirms the possibility of redemption from evil and even overcoming evil itself through self-sacrifice. It is a symbol of great strength and resilience.

The Cape

The black mantle represents menacing, awful darkness to the Outer, hiding an avenging force always prepared to burst out against the Evil Ones.

The Banner of the West

The Banner of the West completes the symbols of the A∴ A∴. It is thus explained in the Zelator Grade: "The White Triangle refers to the three Paths connecting Malkuth with the other Sephiroth; while the Red Cross is the Hidden Knowledge of the Divine Nature which is to be obtained through their aid. The Cross and the Triangle together represent Life and Light." It also represents eternally the possibility of rescuing the Evil. Still, the Tiphareth Cross (6 squares) is placed within the White Triangle of the Supernals, representing that Sacrifice is made only unto the Higher. In this instance, the red

Cross is bordered with gold to represent the Perfect Metal obtained in and through the Darkness of Putrefaction. Black is its field, which thus represents the Darkness and Ignorance of the Outer, while the White Triangle again symbolizes the Light shining in the Darkness but not comprehended. Therefore, the Banner of the West symbolizes Twilight as it is, the equation of Light and Darkness. The pole and the base are black to show that, even in the depths of Evil, that symbol can stand. The cord is black, but the transverse bar and the lance-point may be gold or brass and the tassels scarlet, similar to the Banner of the East, to symbolize Divine Self-renunciation, whose trials and sufferings are, in essence, the Ornament of the Completed Work.

OPENING & CLOSING OF
THE NEOPHYTE RITUAL

Office and Station of the A-n

The A-n's station is on the throne of the West, symbolizing the ebb and flow of darkness and light. The A-n's office is strength. The A-n's office and station correspond to the Sephirah Malkuth on the Tree of Life.

The position of the Throne of the West lies at the lowest point of Malkuth. It is appropriate for the Avenger of the Gods because he or she is placed there in eternal affirmation against the Evil One. The Throne is also positioned there as a seat of witness and punishment decreed against Evil. The Throne serves two functions: to prevent the Qlippoth from entering and to stop anyone lingering outside this area from entering out of curiosity.

The three main ritual officers (EA, A-n, and A-t) correspond to the three stages of the alchemical process. The Black Work represents the Preparation and Putrefaction phase of the alchemical operation. It starts with appearances as they are. It focuses on breaking down and dissolving forms. Therefore, it is symbolized by the A-n and his or her black mantle. As a sign of destruction, the A-n's sword signifies the beginning steps in learning and practicing the occult.

The purpose of practical occultism is to help us go beyond the usual limits of our personality and become more than just ordinary humans. We cannot do this without leaving behind our old self. Mystic death must come before occult resurrection. There is no way to become a true occultist without making deep changes to our personality. This often trips up many people. Those who study occultism and join occult societies are often driven by a desire to change their circumstances. They want to gain powers. They want to learn how to do wonders. But they often resist changing themselves. Therefore, the address of the A-n should be carefully studied and reflected upon by every Neophyte, and it might be helpful for some members of higher grades to review it from time to time. The main message of this address is the A-n's advice that the Neophyte adopt a mental state worthy of this Order. His or her closing words about perseverance reinforce the idea that the main goal of occult work is to transform the operator's personality.

Oration

During the oration, the A-n holds the sword in his or her right hand, extending it at a 45-degree angle. At the line, "So may it be," EA lowers his or her scepter, and A-n dips his or her sword simultaneously.

Secret Name

This is a secret of the order; therefore, two paragraphs were omitted.

Antiphony

The antiphony occurs after the declaration of the secret name. It begins with the words Alpha and Omega, the Greek names for the letters we call A and O. These words are spoken by the same officers who say these letters in the declaration of the secret name — and for the same reason. Additionally, the mystery teaching has been passed down to us from the Orient through Egypt and was originally formulated in Greek. These letters, in the Christian Revelation of St. John, also appear elsewhere in ancient mystery texts, including fragments of rituals from the Eleusinian Mysteries.

Mystic Circumambulation

The A-n, whose office corresponds to the 4 = 7 grade of the First Order, follows the Second Order members during Mystic Circumambulation, symbolizing the highest level of knowledge and skill to be attained in the First Order.

During the Mystic Circumambulation, the A-n carries the sword in the right hand at heart level. As he or she passes the East during the Mystic Circumambulation, he or she dips the sword, visualizing that it is receiving a portion of the current of light streaming out through the tip of the EA's scepter, in recognition of the idea that the powers represented by the insignia owe whatever efficacy they have to the secret virtue of the East specialized in those powers. The A-n needs to dip the sword before passing the East and keep it lowered until it has passed the East.

The A-n passes the EA once and continues with the procession until arriving at his or her throne, then leaves the procession and stands facing East, holding the sword extended upward at a 45-degree angle. The tip of the sword should point toward the tip of the EA's scepter, and the A-n should imagine that the sword is receiving light streaming from the scepter's tip.

The A-n, the Avenger of the Gods, inherits the Light; therefore, he or she only passes the EA once.

Adoration

The A-n holds the sword as in the Oration and dips at the end of each line. At the "Amen," the Sign of Silence is given by the left hand.

It is a helpful visualization to see the image of the Sun reflected in the sword each time it is dipped, as if, through this image, the sword receives an impression of the true nature of this Lord, who is the "interior Sun" of each of us.

Declaration and Mystic Words

After the Adept commands the H-r to declare that he or she has opened, the Lodge is signaled by a single knock from the EA, which the A-n and the A-t repeat. This confirms the establishment of the White Triangle and the completion of the Opening Ceremony. Afterwards, the mystic words accompanying the knocks seal the image of the Light.

Reverse Circumambulation

The Reverse Circumambulation aims to withdraw the Light. After passing the EA once, the A-n continues with the procession until reaching his or her throne, then leaves the procession and stands facing East, holding the sword extended upward at a 45-degree angle. The sword's tip should be pointed at the tip of the EA's scepter, and the A-n should imagine that the sword sends the light it received back to the EA's scepter.

THE RITE OF INITIATION

Note that this entire ritual focuses on a path from outer darkness to inner light. The reception, initial purification, and consecration happen symbolically in the darkest part of Malkuth. When this is complete, the candidate's aura is purified and consecrated. They are led to the foot of the Altar, beneath the citrine part of Malkuth, which receives the impact of the Middle Pillar.

Obligation

A crucial part of the Obligation is wielding the sword by the A-n. The penalty clause of the obligation deserves the Neophyte's utmost attention and deep reflection. It is a penalty that every violator of the obligation imposes upon themselves. No external power enforces punishment. When we forget our pledge, we punish ourselves. Only in the most extreme cases does it operate with the full force described in the closing words of our pledge, but whenever we oppose the current of force with which we are placed in special contact by

Initiation, we experience some degree of the destructive and disintegrating effect, which is always a result of misusing that relation.

First Circumambulation

As the procession passes the A-n, he or she knocks once. This signifies the establishment of a special connection between the candidate and the external cosmic order represented by the A-n. The candidate is, at this point, introduced to a new relationship with all the forces and laws of nature, and if one makes proper use of the opportunities afforded by that contact, they will go far.

Second Circumambulation

The H-r bars the candidate's approach to the West to indicate that nature man cannot understand, even the Darkness, unless through purification and consecration of the physical vessel of the candidate.

As the procession moves toward the West, the candidate catches a glimpse of the Guardian of the West and learns that the Guardian's name is "Darkness." Within this name lie hidden many practical secrets that will be revealed later. Then, the candidate receives their first practical instruction, a warning about fear and its consequences. Notice that this warning comes from an officer who embodies the greatest cause of fear – namely, darkness. It's as if the Adversary is instructing the candidate on how to overcome that very Adversary. This is a profound lesson. In truth, carefully considering whatever appears to oppose us always shows us how it can be overcome even in the most adverse conditions.

When the procession passes the A-n, after his or her words of instruction, he or she knocks to establish a second link between the candidate and the forces that the candidate is to learn to master.

Invocation

The Purifier and the Consecrator stand behind the candidate, left and right respectively; the two and the H-r, positioned at the northeast corner of the altar, form a supporting Triad. The candidate kneels, and the EA advances to a point just east of the altar, where the A-t and the A-n join him/her. The A-t stands on the south side of the altar, facing it, while the A-n faces the altar from the north side. Thus, the EA, A-n, and A-t form the Supernal Triad. They join their insignia as a symbol of the concentration of certain forces over the altar.

As the Adept invokes the Lord of the Universe, all members and officers in the Temple stand to show that through this invocation of the Supreme Power, all inner forces are activated. The invocation itself grants the candidate a special display of power that binds him or her indissolubly to the Inner School or Third Order.

The hoodwink is now loosened, and at the EA's word, it is removed. At the same moment, everyone present sharply claps their hands as a symbol of the change that has been made. From now on, the candidate is no longer called "Child of Earth." He or she has been symbolically reborn, can never stand again in exactly the same relationship to the outer work, and is also admitted to a completely new relationship with the inner forces, of which everything in our Temple are outer symbols.

After removing the hoodwink, the EA, the A-n, and the A-t join scepters and sword above the Neophyte's head, forming the Supernal Triad once more and confirming the new Neophyte's acceptance into the Order.

Antiphony

The three Chief Officers first indicate the W___'s path, then the L___'s path, and finally the path of H_____. The W comes first because of the hidden truth that the universe is mental, and all phenomena originate in the ideas of the Cosmic Mind. The vibration of the WORD manifests the L, and H is the synthesis of both W and L.

Mystic Words

The three Chief Officers then pronounce the mystic words to seal the flow of Light. A knock follows each word and corresponds to one of the nine Sephiroth after Kether in the tenfold manifestation of the Life-Power. This is the point where the magnetic influences of the three officers work together, directing their energy toward the aura of the Neophyte.

Only after being brought to the Light is the Neophyte led to the East of the Altar, which affirms that with this Light, they will be able to cast out and trample on their own Evil Persona. When it is put in its place, it will become a support to them. Therefore, the duty of entrusting the Neophyte with the secret signs, etc., is delegated to the A-n, "The Avenger of the Gods." The A-n is the one who first places the Neophyte between the Pillars and supervises their final purification and consecration. This brings the unique force of the A-n in matter to aid the Neophyte, helping them fight the temptations of the Evil Persona more safely and firmly.

Between the Pillars

The place where the A-n now moves forward to the Neophyte is usually where the A-t typically has his or her seat. The A-n, remember, signifies Malkuth, or the Kingdom. When the Neophyte participates in the "Secrets of the Kingdom," symbolized by the knowledge given to him or her by the A-n, the Neophyte becomes a king. It is, therefore, advanced to the place in the Temple occupied by the King, who is also the Christos.

A-n's Address

The address of the A-n is designed to firmly fix in the mind of the Neophyte the fundamental principles that will govern all his or her subsequent work. The A-n provides this address because it represents the "Kingdom," that is, the system of orderly law which a practical occultist can control to influence the conditions of his or her environment. The words of this address are few; however, the ideas encompass all that is necessary for complete success in our work.

CHAPTER 6 – Duties of the A-n

As the senior 1st Order member of a Lodge, the Archon is not just a figurehead but a leader responsible for overseeing not only "the subordinate officers in the execution of their duties" but all 1st Order members as well. He/she acts as a kind of "den mother/father" for the group. It is your job to ensure that members are informed of the dates and times for Convocation, Attunement, or practice sessions. Phone calls or emails should be made to notify members or remind them of these dates and times. This also helps us estimate how many members to expect. The EA or a Chief will normally notify any candidates for admission or attunements. Your responsibility is to the group as a whole.

While overseeing the group, you will also help set the tone for the convocation. Ensuring there is no unnecessary or loud conversation among members and encouraging them to be in a receptive, meditative state will help maintain the ritual's sacredness. You can also assist by answering questions and providing constructive guidance to anyone who needs it, so the EA isn't unnecessarily disturbed before the convocation. Normally, the EA and 2nd Order members meditate in a different part of the temple before the ritual. Therefore, it's beneficial for the Archon to take on as much responsibility as possible to ensure the preparations for the ritual go smoothly.

Take some time to reflect on what the Archon symbolizes in the temple, including its placement in the West, its grade, and how it interacts with other officers and members. There is no substitute for developing your own connections and interpretations. This will help you become a more effective Archon and deepen your personal experience. It can be helpful to record your experiences in your journal and, perhaps, at the end of your term, to summarize what the role of Archon has meant to you and any insights you've gained. A brief description of the energies perceived by one Archon during her term is included at the end of this section. Sandalphon is the Archangelic energy you are channeling through to the Convocation.

The written copies of the Outer Court and any papers about the Archon are for your eyes only. It is the responsibility and duty of the Archon to give the Outer Court Guided Meditation before each Neophyte Ritual. Remember, you uphold and pass on the Western Mysteries' oral tradition by providing the Outer Court work before the ritual. Using either a short or long version is up to you, though the EA may sometimes express their preferences. A good rule of thumb is to do a complete, long version of the Outer Court on the first meeting after an Initiation, so new members can hear and become familiar with the scene. Do a shorter version at meetings where a long evening is scheduled, or if you believe a brief version benefits the group. At the Equinox, extend your meditation to include a more festive tone and to encompass many other Initiates, whether living or past. Have a large astral group present.

You are asked to write your version of the Outer Court. Expand on the outline to reflect your personal view of the scene. In past experiences, you have no doubt visualized the images in your mind along with the rest of the group. This is your chance to retell this story from your perspective. As emphasized, unity of thought is vital in forming the group mind. Your version must be approved by the Prolocutor and reviewed by the current EA. This ensures we're all aligned in thought and images. Useful elements to include in your version are smells, sounds, colors, textures, and other sensory details.

It is better to perform the Outer Court as a real-time visualization rather than just reading it. You will notice small differences in details each time you work on it during Convocation, helping you understand the main points while remaining open to slight variations in sensory experiences. At first, you might read your script or follow an outline. As you become more comfortable with this method, the visualization will become more vivid – something the group will also notice. If needed, you can keep using an outline to ensure you cover the main points and stations accurately. The invocations are standard and must be used. Feel free to read them aloud. A pitch pipe or chimes can be helpful for tuning the notes, or you might come up with another creative method.

In your preparation for the work, taking time to analyze and understand the steps we take before entering the temple is worthwhile. Each "stop" along the way holds special significance. This will greatly enhance your visualization when it's time to share it with the group.

Discuss the role and the Outer Court with the outgoing Archon. He or she can answer questions or provide relevant advice.

The Archon Notebook and any documents from the Outer Court and other Archon duties will be returned to the Cancellarius at the end of your term. Also, at the end of your term, please add your printed version of the Outer Court to the Archon's notebook.

THE OUTER COURT

(Short version) Adapted by Soror S.

It's late in the afternoon and warm. We've traveled a long way over the past few weeks and have once again arrived in this seaport city on the edge of the desert, over 2000 years ago. We walk to the marketplace and hear the familiar sounds – the friendly chatter, footsteps, and the music of flutes. We smell the scent of baked bread and exotic incense. We walk purposefully toward our destination; there's no time to linger today. As we approach the "Court of the Seekers,' passing through the gate, we notice the inscription above that reads, "Know Thyself."

We enter the "Garden of Mysteries" and find it just as we remembered: beautiful and peaceful, with the scent of sweet orange and rose blossoms. We are hot and uncomfortable from traveling, but the cool, refreshing air of this ancient garden provides relief. We remove our dusty cloaks and instantly feel free from all our worries, concerns, and fears from the outside world. Moving toward the Pyramid of the Sun in the distance, which is brilliantly reflected by the setting sun, we start down the stone path toward it and begin our preparations.

First, we approach the Altar of Burnt Offerings and pause to sprinkle handfuls of bitter myrrh over the red coals. We don't need our negative emotions in this sacred space, so we symbolically set them aside.

We move to the laver of brass and splash the crystal-clear, cool waters of purification on our faces and arms. We know we have been purified for the work ahead. Our white robes are laid out for us, and we put them on, feeling the soft caress of the loose folds against our skin. We are now dressed for labor and pass through the large, free-standing portal into the presence of the four sphinxes.

As we recall, they are lying on their stomachs, paws outstretched in the classic pose of the Great Sphinx of Egypt. The two on the right have the heads of a lion and a man; the two on the left have heads of an ox and an eagle. We pass between them to the Altar of Incense. We pause to reflect on our spiritual goals and recommit ourselves to the Great Work by casting handfuls of sweet frankincense onto the simmering coals.

Our preparations are complete, and we gather at the foot of the seven steps leading up to the temple's portico. We are ready to chant the invocations, and we form a circle, holding hands.

We invoke Thee, O Who art the Highest, the Source, the One Unity, O **EHEIEH**. (E C F C)

From the One Source flows the vital, radiant Life-energy of the Universal Father, the Ensouler of all forms. We invoke Thee, O **YOD-HEH-VAU-HEH**.
(F C C# C)

From the Father, the Light is taken by the Universal Mother, who gives it form and pattern, the Organizer of all Life. We invoke Thee, O *ELOHIM*. (E F# C F G#)

The Mother directs her organic patterns of Life-energy to the Lord of the Earthsphere, who shapes them into the living bodies that populate the Universe. We invoke Thee, O **ADONAI** (E F# G F).

We observe the temple entrance as the massive double brass doors slowly swing open. Out steps the noble Sar Shalom, Guardian of the temple door. His eyes glow with radiance and love as he gazes at us. He signals us to come forward. It is time. We ascend the seven steps (pause). Now, walk with me in silence as we enter the sacred temple of our work.

Outer Court Meditation Outline

Arrival. Use vivid imagery to engage all five senses.

The Gate. Before entering the temple, we peel off layers of clothing. The city's bustle turns into quiet inside the Court of the Seekers.

Garden of Mysteries. The loud, artificial city is replaced by natural scenery. In this safe place, we can remove our cloaks of care and concern.

Altar of Burnt Offerings. The incense myrrh is sacred to Saturn.

Laver of brass. Brass is associated with Venus, and water is linked to the Moon. The two feminine planets are symbolically infusing us with their purification and blessings.

The Four Sphinx are the guardians of Tiphareth's inner temple.

Altar of Incense. The incense frankincense is sacred to the Sun and is associated with Tiphareth. This invokes our personal indwelling Christos and then dedicates our aspirations to this presence.

The seven steps leading to the temple's entrance are where we combine our visualization with reality. As we stand and hold hands, the temple in our minds is the same as the temple in your work.

Other Considerations

While chanting, try to sense your body vibrating as you recite the divine names.

Sar Shalom means Prince of Peace. This is another symbol of Tiphareth.

After finishing the meditation, the Herald enters the temple and informs the EA that the initiates are ready. The Herald makes one last check to ensure the temple is prepared and waits at the door until the EA instructs him to admit the members.

Order of Entrance into the Temple

Herald

Wait for Herald to notify EA and open the portal before the rest of the group goes in.

Purifier
Consecrator
Architect
Archon
4=7 Sr.
0=0
1=10
4=7 Jr.
3=8
2=9

Members provide the semester password to the Herald, then sign in and step forward as a neophyte upon entry.

CHAPTER 7 – Diagrams

The 4=7 Diagrams and Symbols

Illustrations of the Philosophus Ritual Diagrams & Symbols, together with an Explanation

The Fire Tablet

The Tablet of Fire is constructed on the same principle as the Tablet of Earth used in the preceding Grade, but the red of Fire predominates.

The Tablet is used in this Grade's Opening and Closing rituals as the fundamental material for focusing the powers of the Fire element and the entities called Salamanders. The secret of its construction and the method of its use are kept for the Second Order.

ל	ו	ר	כ	י	א	ל	מ	י	כ	א	ל
ע	י	ו	ה	ר	י	נ	ס	ט	נ	ד	ר
ח	פ	ע	ט	א	ו	י	ז	ל	ב	ר	א
ז	ס	ה	י	א	ל	ש	ר	ט	י	ה	ב
י	ז	ר	ה	ב	נ	י	מ	י	א	י	ו
מ	ו	ש	ד	ט	ל	ה	א	נ	ל	ת	ה
ה	ה	ל	ו	ל	ש	ש	ר	א	ס	ל	א
ה	א	א	ה	א	א	ר	י	י	ר	ב	מ
ב	מ	ס	י	ר	א	פ	ה	א	י	ר	ל
ת	ה	ע	ד	נ	ת	ש	ק	ל	ט	מ	כ
א	נ	י	ו	ס	ל	א	ו	ע	י	י	י
ר	ס	נ	ט	ע	ר	ט	ס	ל	א	מ	ר
ש	מ	ר	ה	נ	ס	ו	ל	ר	ז	י	א

The Chaldean Flame Alphabet

The alphabet in which the Tablet of Fire is written is traditionally the Hebrew alphabet. The final forms of the letters are not used when constructing the Fire Tablet.

English				English		
A	Aleph	א		L	Lamed	ל
B	Beth	ב		M	Mem	מ
G	Gimel	ג		N	Nun	נ
D	Daleth	ד		S	Samekh	ס
H	Heh	ה		O	Ayin	ע
V	Vav	ו		P	Peh	פ
Z	Zain	ז		Ts	Tzaddi	צ
Ch	Cheth	ח		Q	Qoph	ק
Th	Teth	ט		R	Resh	ר
Y,I	Yod	י		Sh	Shin	ש
K	Kaph	כ		Tv	Tav	ת

29th Path Admission Badge

Cross of the Zodiac

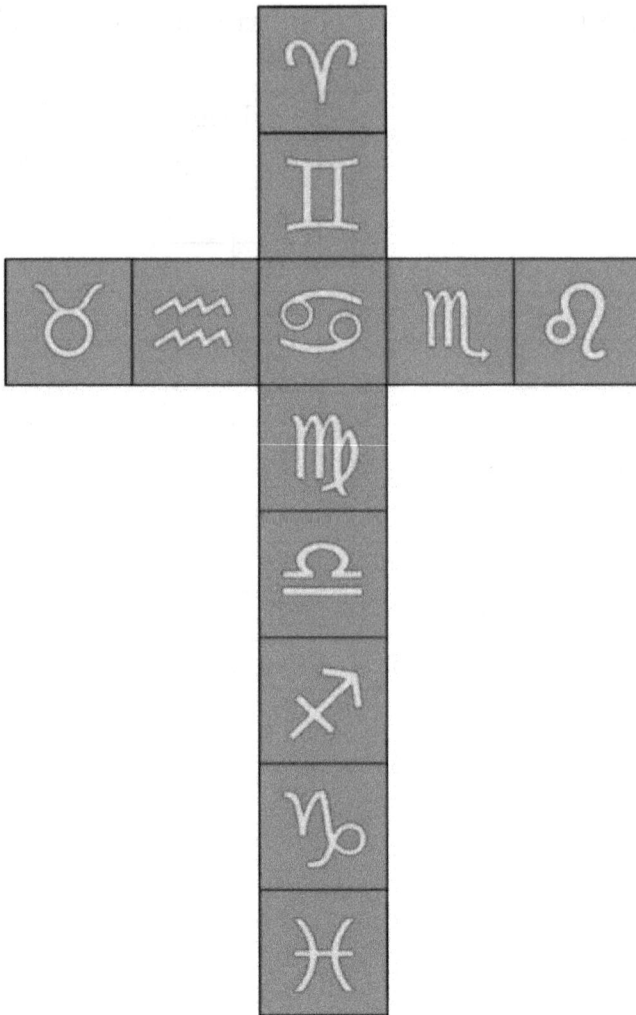

The Cross of 12 Squares symbolizes the zodiac, which includes the Waters above the Firmament. It also hints at the eternal River of Eden, divided into four parts, matching the four triplicates of the zodiac.

The Tarot Key for the 29th Path is Key 18, The Moon. Key 18 symbolizes the inner meaning of the 29th Path.

This depicts the Moon, with 18 Hebrew Yods falling like dew drops. A dog and a wolf, two towers, a path leading to a distant height, and in the foreground, water with a crayfish crawling toward the land complete the symbolism.

The Moon is waxing on the side of Mercy. From it, 16 principal and 16 secondary rays emanate, making a total of 32 Paths of Wisdom.

The battlemented towers represent the conflicting, combative forces presented to the human mind by the appearances of the sphere of sensation.

Beyond them lies a path, ascending toward the heights of spiritual achievement and understanding, the Mystic Mountain of our ancient Brethren of the Rosy Cross.

A wolf and a dog guard it. Both are members of the same genus. Both symbolize the desire-nature, which is the special task of the Philosophus to use and guide in his or her progress toward the Highest Good.

The crayfish emerging from the pool illustrates how Corporeal Intelligence initially appears in forms that naturally inhabit water. Some link this crayfish to the ancient Egyptian god Khephra, a symbol of the Sun below the horizon, as it always is when the Moon rises above.

Careful inspection of this Key will reveal to the Philosophus that its symbolism is rooted in the ancient Qabalistic aphorism: "First the stone, then the plant, then the animal and then the man." All of these are depicted in the section of the design on the near side of the towers. Beyond them, the path leads to "more than man," the true Stone of the Wise.

28th Path Admission Badge

Cube of Balanced Forces

The Admission Badge of this Path is the Cube of Balanced Forces. It symbolizes the Divine Name, Yod Heh Vav Heh, because it has six faces, eight corners, and twelve edges, so the sum of the numbers needed to define its proportions is 26, the number of the Name, Yod Heh Vav Heh.

Because every face of a cube is equal to any other face, so any one of the six sides can serve as its base, the cube has long been a symbol of truth.

This truth reveals itself to man during meditation; thus, the cube is directly connected to the meanings of the 28th Path.

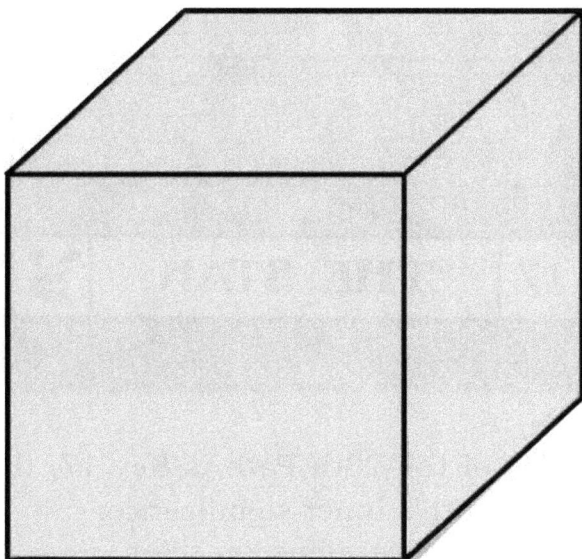

The Tarot Key of the 28th Path is Key 17, the Star. It represents the path's inner significance.

The large star in the sky has eight main rays and eight secondary rays. This symbolizes the Ogdoad multiplied by the Dyad, resulting in the number 16. This corresponds to the Hebrew verb *ha.vaw* (הוה), which primarily means "to breathe." Therefore, it is one of many symbols representing the Cosmic Life-breath and the element of Air, to which the 28th Path is connected.

Note that the three letters of *ha.vaw* are Heh, Vav, and Heh, forming the final part of the Divine Name, Yod Heh Vav Heh, separated from the Paternal Yod. Thus, the word represents the entire Tree of Life below Chokmah. The first Heh corresponds to Binah; the Vav represents the six Sephiroth that make up the Lesser Countenance; and the final Heh corresponds to Malkuth.

The connection of this word to the great star in Key 17 establishes the latter as a symbol of all the powers of manifested existence, represented on the Tree of Life by the eight Sephiroth from Binah to Malkuth, inclusive.

Surrounding the large star are seven smaller stars. Each has eight points to indicate that each shares the same essential nature as the larger one. These seven inner stars represent the seven alchemical metals and the seven Sephiroth from Binah to Yesod.

The nude figure represents the unveiled Isis or Venus-Urania. Therefore, she embodies the power that governs the activities of the Seventh Sephirah, which corresponds to the Grade of Philosophus. She is also Aima, Binah, and Tebunah, the Great Supernal Mother,

Aima Elohim, pouring the waters of creation onto the Earth.

The two urns hold the influences of Chokmah and Binah. Her right hand activates the powers of the ninth sephirah, Yesod, symbolized by the pool. Her left vase is divided into five streams, representing the Quintessence, the four elements, and the subtle principles of sensation.

The bird of Hermes, resting on the tree to her right, represents the powers of Hod, the Eighth Sephirah. The kneeling woman, a symbol of Venus, corresponds to the energies in Netzach and is therefore positioned to the right of the center of the design.

The mountain in the background represents the Great Work and the Mystic Mountain of our ancient Brethren of the Rosy Cross.

27th Path Admission Badge

Cross of Ten Squares

The Cross of Ten Squares represents the Ten Sephiroth in balanced arrangement, before which the formless and void rolled back. It is also the open form of the double cube and the Altar of Incense.

		1 כתר		
3 בינה	**5** גבורה	**6** תפארת	**4** חסד	**2** חכמה
		7 נצח		
		8 הוד		
		9 יסוד		
		10 מלכות		

The Tarot Key for the 27th Path is Key 16, The Star. Key 16 symbolizes the inner significance of the 27th Path.

It depicts a tower struck by lightning, emerging from a rayed circle and ending in a triangle. This lightning bolt symbolizes the Flaming Sword, as explained in a previous Grade. Note that the circle and lightning resemble the astronomical symbol for Mars.

The tower symbolizes the Tower of Babel. It is constructed of twenty-two layers of brick, representing the aspects of human speech when that speech is rooted in the false belief of separateness, embodied by the solitary peak upon which the tower stands.

The scene illustrates the storm, aligning with the themes in the three Chief Officers' ritual speeches. Hidden within this symbolic language is the state of ignorance and confusion that occurs before the truth is revealed. Here lies the hidden meaning of the ancient Qabalistic teaching about the Kings of Edom.

Three holes are torn in the tower's walls, symbolizing the Triad's presence inside.

On the right side of the picture are ten Hebrew Yods arranged in the shape of the Tree of Life diagram. They represent the powers of the letters from Aleph to Yod, inclusive. On the other side of the tower are twelve Yods arranged to resemble the outline of Figure 8 or Ogdoad. They symbolize the letters from Kaph to Tav, inclusive.

Note that these 22 Yods hang, as it were, in the air. The purpose of this is that the essential powers of Being represented by the Hebrew letters are self-supporting and have no material foundation other than themselves.

Admission Badge for the 26th Path.

The Red Calvary Cross

This Cross, already familiar to you, also symbolizes Tiphareth, Netzach, Hod, and Yesod, resting upon Malkuth. It also represents the pattern of the Cube and is known as the 6 Sephiroth of the Microprosopus, symbolizing the balance of cosmic forces.

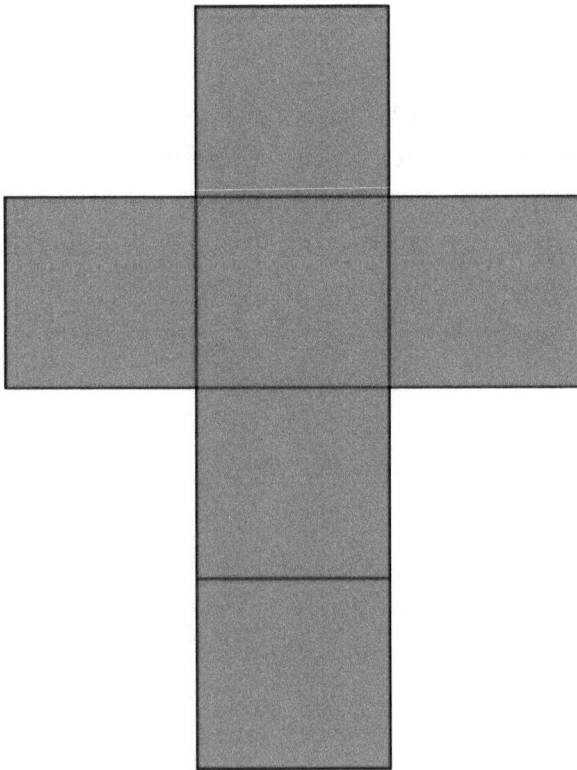

THE GARDEN OF EDEN AFTER THE FALL

This is the symbolic representation of the Fall. For the Great Goddess, who in the Grade of Practicus was supporting the columns of the Sephiroth, in the sign of the Grade of Theoricus, being tempted by the Tree of Knowledge (whose branches, indeed, tend upward into the seven lower Sephiroth but also extend downward into the Kingdom of Shells), reached down to the Qlippoth, and immediately the columns were left unsupported. The Sephirotic System was shattered, and Adam, the Microprosopus or Lesser Countenance, fell with it.

Then the great Dragon with seven heads and ten horns arose, and the Garden was left desolate. Malkuth was separated from the Sephiroth by his intersecting folds and linked to the Kingdom of the Shells. The seven lower Sephiroth were cut off from the Three Supernals in Da'ath, at the feet of Aima Elohim.

And because in Da'ath there was the greatest rise of the great Serpent of Evil, there is, as it were, another Sephirah, making the infernal or averse Sephiroth eleven instead of ten. And Da'ath, having developed a new head in the Dragon, the Seven-headed Dragon with ten horns became an eight-headed and eleven-horned creature.

Therefore, the rivers of Eden were desecrated, and from the Dragon's mouth, the infernal waters flowed into Da'ath. And this is Leviathan, the crooked serpent.

But between the devastated Garden and the Supernal Eden, Yod Heh Vav Heh Elohim placed the letters of the Name and the Flaming Sword so that the highest part of the Tree of Life would not be involved in the Fall of Adam. Therefore, it was necessary for the Second Adam to come and restore all things. Just as the First Adam was crucified on the Cross of the Celestial Rivers, the Son had to be crucified on the Cross of the Infernal Rivers of Da'ath. To accomplish this, he first had to descend to the lowest point, even to Malkuth.

MAGIC SQUARE AND KAMEA OF VENUS

Magic Square						
22	47	16	41	10	35	4
5	23	48	17	42	11	29
30	6	24	49	18	36	12
13	31	7	25	43	19	37
38	14	32	1	26	44	20
21	39	8	33	2	27	45
46	15	40	9	34	3	28

Kamea						
כב	מז	יו	מא	י	לה	ד
ה	כג	מח	יז	מב	יא	כט
ל	ו	כד	מט	יח	לו	יב
יג	לא	ז	כה	מג	יט	לז
לח	יד	לב	א	כו	מד	כ
כא	לט	ח	לג	ב	כז	מה
מו	יה	מ	ט	לד	ג	כח

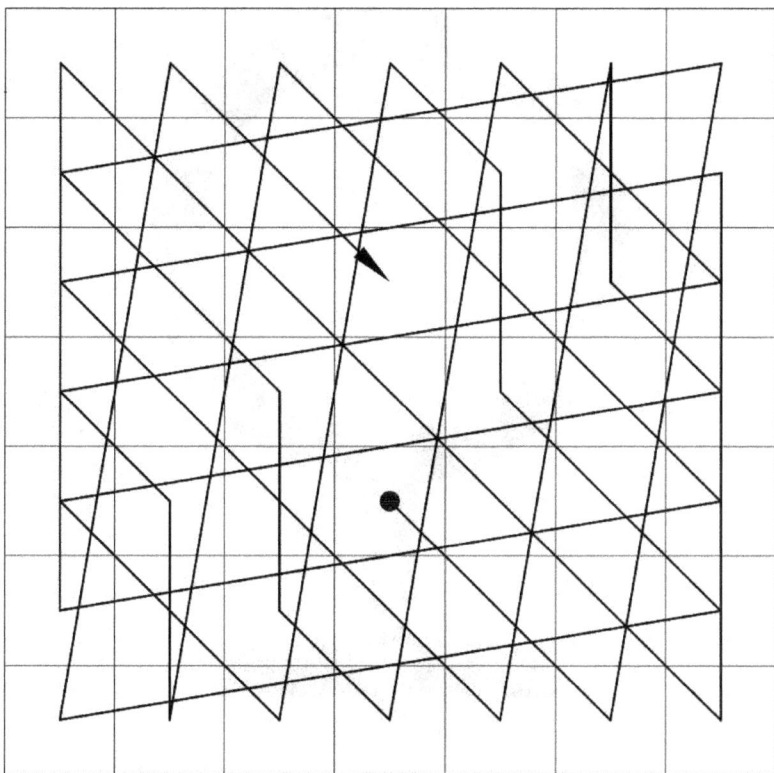

The Grade of Philosophus is associated with the Sphere of Venus, which rules in Netzach, and therefore, the Kamea or Magic Square of Venus and the Magic Line formed are among its symbols. From it are derived the sigils related to the planet Venus and the Divine and Angelic Names connected with it.

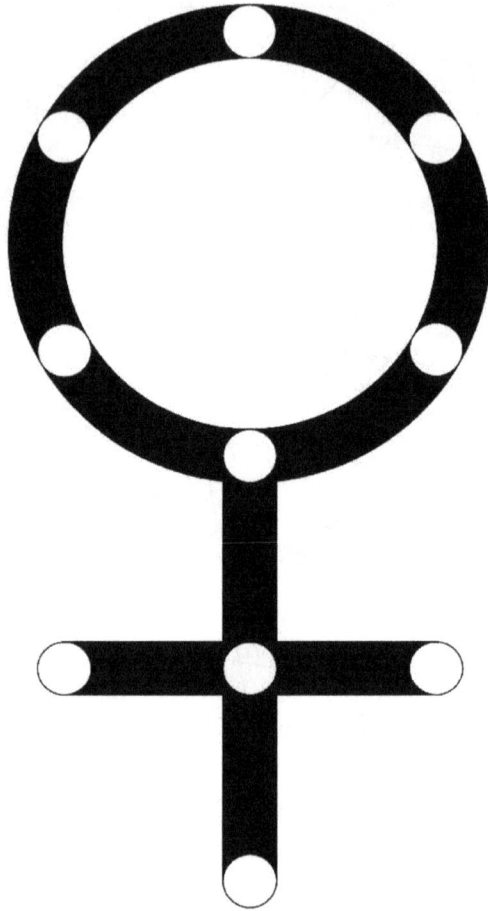

The symbol of Venus, inscribed on the Tree of Life, appears in the diagram before you. It encompasses the entire Sephiroth and is, therefore, a fitting emblem of the Isis of Nature; hence, its circle is larger than Mercury.

TRINITY ON THE TREE OF LIFE

ROOT OF

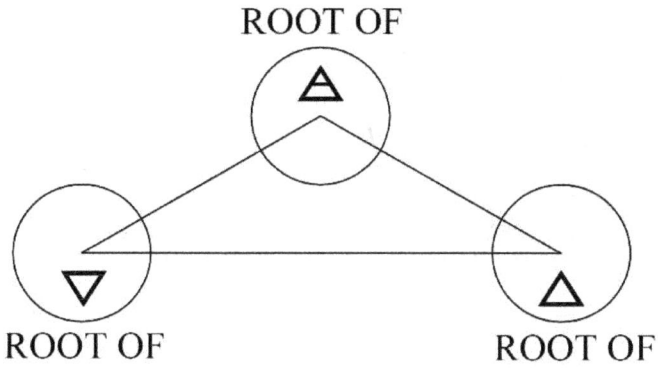

ROOT OF   ROOT OF

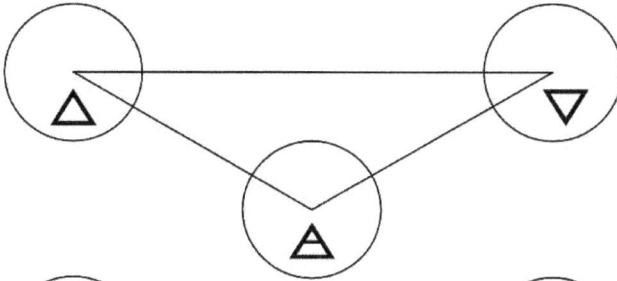

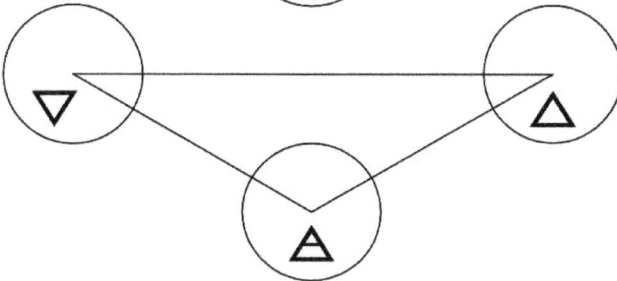

This diagram illustrates the Trinity, or the "Three Mothers," functioning through the Sephiroth and reflected downward into the four triangles of the elements. Kether is the Root of Air, reflected downward from Kether to Yesod through Tiphareth. Chokmah is the Root of Fire, reflected from Chokmah, through Geburah, to Netzach. Binah is the Root of Water, reflected from Binah through Chesed to Hod.

The tenth Sephirah, Malkuth, represents Earth, serving as the receptacle and synthesis of Air, Fire, and Water.

CHAPTER 8 – Correspondences

Qabalistic Correspondences of the Philosophus Grade
Netzach; Fire (Shin); 29th (Qoph),
28th (Tzaddi) and 27th (Peh) Paths

Compiled By Soror S.[1]

NETZACH
(Victory: Venus)

HEBREW & ENGLISH NAME: *Netzach* (נצח), Victory

LOCATION ON THE TREE OF LIFE: At the foot of the
Pillar of Mercy at the right angle of the Triangle of
Personality. Seat of the Desire Nature.

ADDITIONAL TITLE GIVEN TO NETZACH: Firmness

GOD-NAME IN ASSIAH: *Yod Heh Vav Heh Tzabaoth*
(יהוה צבאות), The Lord of Hosts

ARCHANGEL IN ASSIAH: *Haniel* (האניאל), Grace of God

ORDER OF ANGELS: *Elohim* (אלהים), Gods

THE HEAVENS OF ASSIAH (PALACE): *Nogah* (נוגה), The
Sphere of Venus

MAGICAL IMAGE: A beautiful naked woman

SPIRITUAL EXPERIENCE: The Vision of Beauty Triumphant

MYSTIC NUMBER: 28

NUMERIC CORRESPONDENCE IN HEBREW

GEMATRIA: 148

ELEMENT: Fire

PLANET: Venus

HEBREW NAME OF THE PATH: *Sekhel Nistar* (נסתר שכל). Occult (or Hidden) Intelligence

The Thirty-two Paths of Wisdom

The 7th Path is the Hidden Intelligence (Sekhel Nistar). It is the brilliance that enlightens all intellectual abilities visible to the mind's eye and the contemplation of faith.

Tarot Attributions – The four sevens

Seven of Wands – Valor – Third Decan Leo.

Seven of Cups – Illusory Success – Third Decan Scorpio.

Seven of Swords – Unstable effort – Third Decan Aquarius.

Seven of Pentacles – Success unfulfilled – Third decant Taurus.

Primary Color

Green: The yellow of Tiphareth mixes with the blue of Chesed. On the Tree of Life, a triangle forms from the relationship between Tiphareth, Chesed, and Netzach. The complementary color of Netzach, red, is associated with Geburah, which is diagonally opposite Netzach on the Pillar of Severity side of Tiphareth. These color associations offer clues to the relationships among these Sephiroth.

Color in the Four Worlds

In Atziluth (King Color Scale): Amber
In Briah (Queen Color Scale): Emerald green
In Yetzirah (Emperor Color Scale): Bright yellowish green
In Assiah (Empress Color Scale): Olive, flecked with gold

EGYPTIAN GODS: Hathor

GREEK GODS: Aphrodite, Nike

ROMAN GODS: Venus

ANIMALS, REAL & IMAGINARY: Lynx, Oyster, Dove, Sparrow, Raven, all carrion birds.

Plants, Real & Imaginary

Rose: Usually considered the perfect flower by its quality of scent, color, shape and beauty.

Laurel: A fragrant plant associated with victory and used by the ancient Greeks for the Victory Crown.

PRECIOUS STONES: Emerald

SEMI-PRECIOUS STONES: Malachite, Jade, Amber, Coral

METAL: Copper

Incense and Perfumes

Rose

Benzoin: A gum resin used to fix and add body to a scent, featuring a characteristic vanilla note.

Myrtle: For its sweet scent

Red Sandalwood

Vegetable Drugs

Damiana: An aphrodisiac. It was also used to relieve anxiety and promote overall well-being as a general tonic.

Turnera diffusa, or damiana, is a shrub native to southern Texas in the United States, Mexico, Central

America, South America, and the Caribbean. It belongs to the family Passifloraceae. Damiana is a relatively small, woody shrub that produces small, aromatic flowers. – Wikipedia

MAGICAL WEAPONS: Lamp, Girdle, Mirror

MYSTICAL VISION: Vision of Beauty Triumphant

Other Symbols

The Rose; the Dove; the Lamp & Girdle, Fire-wand, Censer; Heptagon & Heptagram

VIRTUE: Unselfishness

VICE: Unchastity, Lust

CORRESPONDENCE IN THE MICROCOSM (HUMAN BODY): Loins, hips, legs

TYPICAL DISEASE: Skin troubles.

PSYCHOLOGICAL CORRESPONDENCE: Desire

RAY: The Power Ray

SHIN (Fire)

The element of Fire is linked to the Grade of Philosophus. These correspondences relate to the Mother letter, Shin, which symbolizes Fire.

The 29th Path – Qoph

HEBREW & ENGLISH NAME: *Qoph* (קף). Back of the Head

HEBREW LETTER: Qoph (ק)

HEBREW LETTER VALUE: 100

PATH ON THE TREE OF LIFE: The 29th Path connecting Malkuth to Netzach

GOD-NAME IN ASSIAH: *El* (אל); *H.H.I.V.* (ההיו)

ARCHANGEL: *Amnitziel* (אמניציאל)

THE HEAVENS OF ASSIAH: *Daggim* (דגים), Pisces

ELEMENT: Water

HEBREW NAME OF THE PATH: *Sekhel Mugsham* (מוגשם שכל), Corporal Intelligence

The Thirty-two Paths of Wisdom

The 29th Path is Physical Intelligence (Sekhel Mugsham). It describes and establishes the development of all physical bodies associated with the Zodiac.

TAROT ATTRIBUTIONS: Key 18, The Moon

ZODIACAL SIGN: Pisces

PRIMARY COLOR: Red-violet

Color in the Four Worlds

King Scale: Red-violet

Queen Scale: Buff, flecked silver-white

Emperor Scale: Light translucent pinkish-brown

Empress Color Scale: Stone color

MUSICAL NOTE: B

PLANETARY RULER: Combined rulership of Jupiter and Neptune

CUBE OF SPACE: South Below

EGYPTIAN GODS: Khephra (symbolizing, in this context, the Sun's silent journey through the darkness of Night and the bitterness of Winter.)

GREEK GODS: Poseidon, Hermes Psychopompos

ROMAN GODS: Neptune

ANIMALS, REAL & IMAGINARY: Beetle, Crayfish, Fish, Jackal, Dog, Dolphin

PLANTS, REAL & IMAGINARY: Unicellular Organisms, Mangrove, Opium, Birthwort

PRECIOUS STONES: Pearl

Incense and Perfumes

Ambergris: Ambergris has a musty, musky scent reminiscent of the sea, subtle and smooth.

MAGICAL WEAPONS: Magic Mirror

Magical Powers

Alchemical Multiplication; The Magical Memory; Divination; Bewitchments; Casting Illusions

THE HUMAN BODY: The Feet

TYPICAL DISEASES: Gout

OTHER ATTRIBUTIONS: Organization; Sleep; Body Consciousness

The 28th Path – Tzaddi

HEBREW & ENGLISH NAME: *Tzaddi* (צדי). Fish Hook

HEBREW LETTER: צ

HEBREW LETTER VALUE: 90

PATH ON THE TREE OF LIFE: The 28th Path connecting Yesod to Netzach

GOD-NAME IN ASSIAH: *IHVH Elohim* (יהוה אלהים)

ARCHANGEL: *Cambriel* (כאמבריאל)

THE HEAVENS OF ASSIAH: *Dali* (דלי), Aquarius

ELEMENT: Air

HEBREW NAME OF THE PATH: *Sekhel Mutba* (מותבע שכל), Natural Intelligence

The Thirty-two Paths of Wisdom

The 28th Path is called Natural Intelligence. It completes and perfects the nature of everything that exists under the Sun's revolution.

TAROT ATTRIBUTIONS: Key 17, The Star

ZODIACAL SIGN: Aquarius

PRIMARY COLOR: Violet

Color in the Four Worlds

King Scale: Violet

Queen Scale: Sky Blue

Emperor Scale: Bluish mauve

Empress Color Scale: White, tinged purple

MUSICAL NOTE: A#

PLANETARY RULER: Combined rulership of Uranus and Saturn

CUBE OF SPACE: South Above

EGYPTIAN GODS: Hapi, Aroueris

GREEK GODS: Hera, Athena, Ganymede

ROMAN GODS: Juno, Aeolus

Animals, Real & Imaginary

Eagle (as Kerub of Air); Peacock (the favorite bird of Juno [Hera], Queen of the gods)

PLANTS, REAL & IMAGINARY: Olive, Coconut, Edderwort, Fennel, Buttercup

PRECIOUS STONES: Amethyst, Star Sapphire

SEMI-PRECIOUS STONES: Lapis Lazuli, Chalcedony

Incense and Perfumes

Galbanum: Its scent is woody, green, tenacious, and slightly balsamic or resinous. The green note imparts an airy quality. Galbanum is related to fennel and is mentioned in the Bible in Exodus 30:34.

Magical Weapons

Censer; Aspergillus (a short-handled implement used for sprinkling holy water)

MAGICAL POWERS: Astrology; Alchemical Dissolution

THE HUMAN BODY: Ankles, calves and lower legs

OTHER ATTRIBUTIONS: Revelation; Meditation

The 27th Path – Peh

HEBREW & ENGLISH NAME: *Peh* (פה), Mouth

HEBREW LETTER: פ

HEBREW LETTER VALUE: 80

GOD-NAME IN ASSIAH: *Elohim Giboor* (אלהים גבור)

ARCHANGEL: *Kamael* (כמאל)

THE HEAVENS OF ASSIAH: *Madim* (מאדים), Mars

ELEMENT: Fire

HEBREW NAME OF THE PATH: *Sekhel Murgash* (מורגש שכל), Exciting Intelligence

The Thirty-two Paths of Wisdom

The 27th Path is the Perceptible or Felt Intelligence. Through it, the senses of all living beings under the zodiac are stimulated.

TAROT ATTRIBUTIONS: Key 16, The Tower

PLANET: Mars

PRIMARY COLOR: Red

Color in the Four Worlds

King Scale: Scarlet
Queen Scale: Red
Emperor Scale: Venetian red
Empress Color Scale: Bright red, rayed azure or emerald

MUSICAL NOTE: C

CUBE OF SPACE: North

EGYPTIAN GODS: Horus

GREEK GODS: Ares, Athena

ROMAN GODS: Mars

ANIMALS, REAL & IMAGINARY: Horse, Bear, Wolf, Boar

PLANTS, REAL & IMAGINARY: Absinthe, Rue, Nut, Galangal, High John Conqueror

PRECIOUS STONES: Ruby

SEMI-PRECIOUS STONES: Garnet, Pyrite, any red stone

METAL: Iron

INCENSE AND PERFUMES: Pepper, Dragon's Blood, all hot, pungent odors

MAGICAL WEAPONS: Sword

MAGICAL POWERS: Destruction of thoughts

THE HUMAN BODY: Muscular system

TYPICAL DISEASES: Inflammation

OTHER ATTRIBUTIONS: Awakening; Grace and Sin

Chapter 8 Notes

[1] A member of the Order compiled the correspondence for the Zelator and Philosophus grades. Soror S was a Grand Chief from my lodge. The correspondences for Practicus and Theoricus were borrowed from another order. Soror S edited and rewrote much of the grade work during her tenure. Before her, the grade work consisted of a mix of handwritten and typed copies. Soror S is one of the unsung heroes of the Order.

CHAPTER 9 – The Fire Wand

By Soror S

The final tool on The Magician's working table is the Fire Wand. The Wand is a symbol of Power. This instrument is used for initiation and corresponds to the plane of Atziluth, where Everything begins to manifest. As a Philosophus, you are now prepared to take on the responsibility of working with your Fire nature, and your magical weapon is the Fire Wand.

The suit of Wands corresponds to the Fire Wand. You might want to examine the Wands suit in your Tarot deck to understand the forces they represent. Each Wand relates to a Sephirah on the Tree of Life, and you'll see that the elemental forces of Fire are present on all levels of your being. The Wand is Yod in the Tetragrammaton, and it also embodies the fiery initiating power of that letter.

The forces of Fire are both projective and creative. To understand them, start by examining how you express Fire. This is easiest to notice in anger, but more importantly, it appears in your "drive to do." Your Fire is your creative energy. It pushes you forward in your quest for the Quintessence. Without it, you would remain "as is," and eventually, your inner flame would cool down. Keeping your flame alive and directed toward positive goals is one of the experiences of the 4=7 Grade. Your Wand will serve as a reminder of the importance of burning the flame and beginning transformation. The meditative practice of creating your own Fire Wand will support you, inspiring and motivating you on your journey of magical transformation.

You should craft a Fire Wand during the Grade of Philosophus and use it as a meditation tool. More detailed instructions will be provided for its use in a later grade, so for now, familiarize yourself with your wand thoroughly. Allow it to guide you in meditation. Let it spark thoughts and ideas that lead to new insights. Your connection to the Fire Wand is vital to its power and importance, making you an essential part of the magical process.

You can deepen your meditational experience by handling your wand near fire or heat. If you have a fireplace, consider holding your wand and contemplating the connection between it and the fire. On a hot day, you might take it outside to feel the power of the heat. Indoors, light candles and watch their flames, imagining them as the fire in your heart. If you sense elemental salamanders, observe their activity. State your intention (as every good Magician should!) and share that you plan to use your Fire Wand to help in the Reign of Light and Harmony in this world, in the name of YOD HEH VAV HEH TZABAOTH. Enjoy the qualities of fire and heat, and remember you can work directly with this force in the extension of LVX!

Meditate regularly with your Fire Wand and record your experiences. Keep this practice going during the Grade of 4=7.

Fire Wand Construction Instructions

The staff of the Wand should be made of wood, round and smooth, perforated from end to end. A magnetized steel rod is placed inside the wand, just long enough to extend 1/16 inch beyond each wooden end. It may be helpful to make the wand from a cane, which naturally has a hollow. If you use a cane, there should be three natural sections based on the knots. If you use wood, place three rings evenly spaced along the shaft.

The wand should be no longer than 18 inches, and a good rule of thumb is the length of your forearm from elbow to wrist.

The top end of the wand should be cone-shaped. This part can be crafted on a lathe, or you might find a suitably shaped piece at a craft store.

A magnetized rod should have a strong charge when inserted into the hollow of the wand. Use a thin rod, like a wire coat hanger, and magnetize it with a magnet. The North end of the magnet should be placed at the bottom of the wand.

The entire wand is painted flame red and divided into three sections by yellow knots or rings. The cone is red with three wavy yellow Yods on it. You will do additional painting on the wand in a later grade, so don't finish it with a heavy topcoat now.

Additional Instructions

You can buy a Fire Wand online from the Golden Dawn Shop. I recommend choosing an unpainted one and doing the work yourself.

Names on the Fire Wand

God Name: IHVH Tzabaoth (יהוה צבאות)

Archangel: Micheal (מיכאל)

Angel: Aral (אראל)

Ruler: Seraph (שרף)

River of Paradise (Fire): Pison (פישון)

Cardinal direction (South): Darom (דרום)

Hebrew name of Fire: Esh (אש)

Your magical motto (aspiration name):

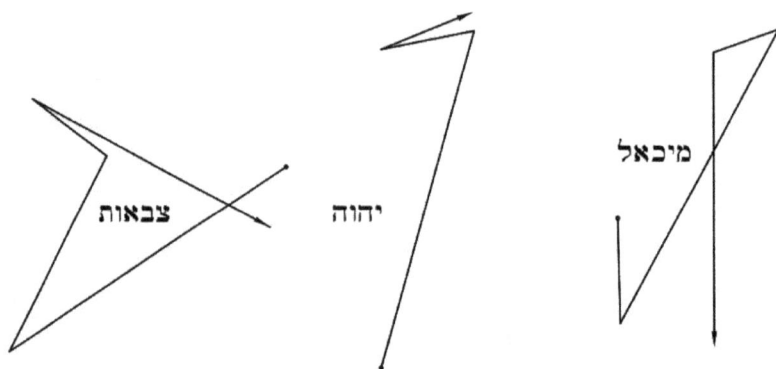

IHVH Tzabaoth

Micheal

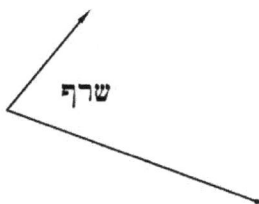

Aral   Seraph   Pison

דרום

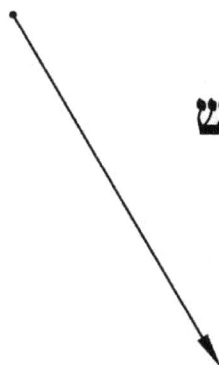

אש

Darom   Esh

CHAPTER 10 - The Unreserved Dedication

By Dolores Ashcroft-Nowicki

Time and time again, there come to the doors of the Mysteries, eager and well-intentioned students offering the unreserved dedication of their lives in service to the Light. It is one of the laws of the Inner Planes that such a dedication is always taken up, even if, as in many cases, the Dedicand is quite unaware of what will be involved in making good such an offer. Then, when the tests come, as they invariably do (for the Adepti take nothing without testing it to the limit), the unexpectedness and weight of the ordeals can cause bewilderment, anger and resentment, and finally apathy and withdrawal.

It is not that the Inner Plane teachers are callous - far from it - but they are bound by their laws to test all who come to them, and those who come prematurely are asking for tasks and tests much heavier than they can bear at that time. As the soul grows stronger, so do the tests become more keen and searching until the dross is burnt away, and the pure gold of the Divine Spark is fully revealed. But as in any undertaking involving lifetimes of work, the tasks of the Mysteries should be approached in graduated steps. We are all in various stages of our journey and progress in each life as far as possible. There is no panic, no prize given to the first, no stigma attached to the last.

At any point in your training, you can say, 'I will stop here - I feel I have gone as far as I can go this time.' This self-honesty is not a sign of failure but a mark of a soul well on the way to true self-knowledge, the *gnothi seauton* [know thyself] of the Ancients. It is said that it takes three lives to make an initiate; in each life, one progresses swiftly to the point last reached, and then the soul surges ahead to the next stage. Once initiation has been achieved, the soul may proceed at its own pace. There may be lives when one regresses, but gradually, one will ascend to the Light. Remember, spiritual growth is a gradual process, and there is no need to rush.

It is usually in the last of three lives of preparation that the unreserved dedication is made, then the tests that follow are the Soul's initiation and how it responds to the tests decides the grade at which its real work will start. Please do not confuse the Initiation of the Soul with the earthly initiations that can be obtained in the body; these are not to be despised, for they also require training and dedication to be achieved. Sometimes, earthly initiation will come first, and sometimes, the spiritual one. But if you receive one, the other will eventually recognize it. It is somewhere between these two points that the unreserved dedication is made. In the full knowledge of what it entails and where it will lead. The total giving of oneself to the Light, without counting the cost it may entail. Remember, your efforts will not go unnoticed and will eventually be recognized.

Sometimes, the force of the Higher Self manifesting at this time is so intense, so one-pointed, that it overrides the personality completely, and this is how the fires of martyrdom are lit. In the past, there have been many such occasions. In our own time, men and women suffer and sometimes die for an ideal that utterly discounts what the conscious mind wants or has to say. But death is not always the test demanded; the tests are not just tests of faith. There is no waste on the Inner Planes. They use the test to refine the soul and wipe out the accrued karma of the past. So the tests not only prove the soul's worth but they clean it up at the same time. There is no place in the Mysteries for the lazy, the self-deluded, the fashionable dabbler or the inflated ego. This is no game we are playing - the aim is too high; our long-hidden divinity is the goal to which we aspire, not only for ourselves but for the whole of our life wave. It is very nice to wander about with flowers in your hair and love in your heart for all, expecting handouts, but don't forget that Western man has to work to learn the discipline of the Earth-Plane. Sharing your possessions with everyone is alright so long as you don't help yourself to the possessions of those who do not subscribe to your beliefs.

White robes and unwashed feet do not constitute sainthood. Learn to live with simplicity, accept and learn the lesson hidden in every experience that comes to you. Move quietly and without haste in your chosen path. Aim for a signpost that is within reasonable reach. Tread firmly on the black squares of life and joyfully on the white squares. Then, one day, instead of a signpost, you will find an altar and know that it is time for you to make the ultimate offering IF YOU SO WISH. If you would rather bide your time, you may do so until you can make that offering. Once the offer is made, pass it on and accept whatever comes, knowing you are being closely watched and that the outcome is being assessed. You will find many companions – some of them unlikely – but all known by their serenity and the love that shines on them.

Do not despise the preliminary work of the Mysteries, though it may seem dull and repetitious, for if you cannot do the dull work, you are not ready for the more exciting work. Carry your training into your earthly life. Make every movement purposeful and meaningful. Learn to enjoy silence and its gift of understanding – if you can be silent with someone, you are in tune with that person. When a student visits us I like to see how long they can sit in silence, and I will sometimes refrain from speaking so that I may ascertain how they can use the silence. Guard the sword of your tongue, not for nothing has it a pointed tip! Without grinding to a halt, learn to slow down the pace of your living and, all the while, tend to the inner flame of the heart. By the sudden surge upward of this flame, you will know when the time for your declaration is near.

Some may be young, married, or about to be so. To you, take your time and tread the Path of the Hearth Fire fully. Study and train by all means, but the life of the Earth-Plane must come first; neglect of the sacred Earth fire will delay you upon the Path, for you will have to come back and tread it again. Many occult schools will not take students under thirty so that they may have stabilized and made sure of their earthly life. Home and work must be on a firm basis. The loving ties between husband and wife, parents and children, must have time to grow and strengthen. All the time, the training will be going on underneath, quietly and without your notice, almost leading you to the time when the Chapel of the Heart can be built on a firm foundation and contact with God within can be made.

We live in an age that no longer uses the rack and stake, but many look at us askance and doubt our view of God. Many class us all under the label of BLACK MAGIC. I do not deny that some study the Mysteries for what they can gain and for self-aggrandizement, but in the School I represent, and in the School I was trained, we work with the Light of the world upon the Altar. Let no one doubt the integrity of our School, for our aim is to return to the Divine Plan put forth by the Creator and bring it to completion. Our ranks are made up of men and women of every race, color and creed. Although our School is based upon Christianity, we do not deny entry to those of other beliefs but welcome them, sincerely believing that there is but one God, one Creator of all life, who goes by many names, and that all humanity is His Children - yes, and all life-forms, for we are part of one whole life wave. Even those who seek to tread the paths of darkness must eventually come to the Light, for He will not turn from them. There is always hope that they will turn aside from the paths of darkness and join us again.

There is always work for the dedicated; for some, it is the comforting and helping of the newly passed over, while others work with the younger brethren of the animal world who give their lives in many ways to man who was set over them. Some work with those sciences the ignorant call the occult, which, when understood, prove to be as natural as electricity. By their work, they push back the frontiers of our knowledge and allay the age-old fears of Magic. Some are called to be teachers, some are withdrawn and work alone, and these are often judged harshly for not being more open. But they are the pioneers who blazed the way for us to follow. Whatever type of occult work you may take up, remember that you carry on a tradition older than the pyramids and just as mysterious.

The outside world may see us as hard, unloving, cold and callous because we do not rage or weep hysterically over the catastrophes and the tragedies that occur daily in this world of speed and violence. But we are aware that there is a wider view of things, we sense a broader scope of a pattern of which we can have only the merest inkling. We cannot hope - at our present stage - to understand the vast plan laid out for us to follow, but at least, as occultists, we are aware that there is a Plan and try (and we can only try) to follow it. Because we do not know the whole of the Divine concept, we realize that we cannot judge and see only a small fraction of that Plan. This kind of knowledge is part of the training of the potential dedicatee. He cannot honestly offer himself and his life energy unless convinced of such a universal pattern. Yet everyone who does reach that point eases the incomprehensible burden of the

Creator. The dedicand is willing and ready to take responsibility for himself and his actions, *for until that moment, God accepts them for him in His love and mercy—every* terrible action. Every hurt, tragedy, pain, horror and terror, God experiences to the full -- not turning away as man does when faced with something too horrible to contemplate. We can turn the pages of the newspaper, turn off the TV, talk about something else, and put it out of our minds somehow, but He goes through it all because the life that suffers is His life; He gave it, and He cares what happens to it. One who makes unreserved dedication accepts responsibility for his actions and any pain resulting from them – the joy that may come to him he shares with all. By that Path, he lifts the heavy burden of the sin and suffering of the world.   That alone is worth the long and arduous training in the Mystery Schools.

The tests we go through are always with a purpose, and not just for their own sake. We always come out of a test with more than we went in with: more faith, more confidence, more ability in our chosen work. The way is never easy at any stage, but such tests are graded, and we are not given more than we can bear. I can testify to this personally. There have been many times when I have felt that I could not go on, that I was unable to cope with what seemed to be not only insurmountable but downright unfair. Somehow, and I have not always known quite how it happened, I have found myself on the other side, in one piece – more or less. There are ways of coping. Some fight their way through the dark valley. Some go cautiously, three steps forward and one back. After a moment's hesitation, some take a few steps forward into the dark and, trusting, hold out a hand. Our hand is always taken, though we may not know whose hand it is at that moment. Thus held, we stumble along until we come to the other side and turn to find that our helper has returned into the darkness to help another. Nothing of value is earned without sacrifice. It would have no value. To those of you who are training in the work of the Mysteries, I would say offer time to your training, offer service to others, offer attention to the great Principles of Creation, and offer what you feel capable of at each point of your training, plus a little more to make it a definite effort. Advance steadily without making a wild dash into the unknown territory. This way, you will not be given tests that are beyond your capacity. Never force yourself on the attention of the Inner Plane teachers, for they will surely send you back until you have learned enough to be useful to them in their work.

There is another aspect to biting off more than you can chew in occultism. You may cause pain and sorrow to your family and others by needlessly incurring a heavy test. There is a marked difference between the Peristyle and the Hypostyle. That difference should not be ignored, at least not until your teacher and the Inner Planes decide that you are ready to offer yourself completely to the Master of Masters. Clear sight is needed -- clear sight and honesty. It sounds wonderful to say, "I have made the Unreserved Dedication," but those who *have* made it rarely admit it. It is too precious to be exposed to those who might mock. Please take it in stages and gradually extend your area of work; first comes your offer of service to your Higher Self, your inner truth principle, the personal Father. There is an offer of service to your school, which is most likely to be needed at this stage. Offer service to your fellow students, and thus will gradually increase your usefulness while preparing for the Highest Offering. Some will find that the smaller service area is sufficient for them and will seek no further. Do not feel superior to them or sorry for them; they have had the inner wisdom to know what they are capable of and the courage to admit it. When the next life comes, they will surge ahead rapidly. There will be those who, in all sincerity, offer Unreserved Dedication and mean it, yet who will, through circumstances beyond their control, be unable to keep it up. Their willingness will count for much and be to their credit; after a while, they may try again and succeed. Some will offer to impress, and they will get short shifts.

Does all this sound as if I am trying to put you off occultism? Dion Fortune once said, "Only the best is good enough for the Masters." The work of the Mysteries and the effect it will have on the future of man demands sincere, well-trained and strong-minded men and women with the ability to stand back from the mass of humanity and survey it with a seemingly dispassionate mind that will, to appearance, belie the unbiased love that lies below the surface. So, you will see, it is no light task. It should not be offered when enthusiastic after seeing an emotive film or reading a book. The Unreserved Dedication is as binding and holy as a priest's ordination. That is just what it is: a Priesthood. For the Higher self brings you to the altar of sacrifice, and the God within lays on the hands of love and healing, and in that moment, the Seeker becomes the Priest. Still with a long way to go, but now with added strength and to spare for others.

If there are those amongst you who are thinking of taking this road, pause and reflect, making sure you are setting out from a good, strong foundation, having fulfilled the Path of the Hearth Fire. Then you can set forth to the goal you have aimed for, the personal quest of the Grail - that Cup which waits on the Altar of the Chapel Perilous for you to win through the wastelands of self, of doubt and the Dark Night of the Soul to where it stands in glory. Knock, and it shall be opened to you. . . but remember, the door can only be opened from the inside - the Chapel Perilous is in your own heart.

Our dreams are but pebbles

She was tossed into the pool of immortality.

CHAPTER 11 – This Troubled World

By Frater C. D.

After traveling a bit along the Path of Return, it's common to experience doubts in our still-early stages. One such doubt is whether our actions are too self-centered and not focused enough on alleviating the world's physical suffering. We often forget that as we become more aware of these pains, feelings of separation from the problems and a sense of selfishness might influence us.

Such a condition can lead to frantic historical research into the factors perpetuating human ills, especially religious ones, along with avid reading of current accounts of horrors and an absorption in the details of social injustice and disorder. Our attention can become focused in this way, even when we know that our subjective processes will inevitably be negatively affected. To avoid this, must we then shut out such awareness and experience an even greater sense of separation, which, in turn, has its subjective repercussions?

With a growing sense of urgency, each generation seeks to restore the previous order and minimize discomfort.

Within the Mystery Teachings, there is a deep care for humanity and an understanding that every soul perceiving life only through the darkness of outward appearances can feel nothing but inner suffering. To ease its fears, it constantly seeks distraction. Because of this, we are encouraged not to focus on outward behavior but to offer compassionate recognition of the troubled and fearful state at the core of the issue.

Humanity has always viewed life as filled with trouble and fear, even when experiencing every social and material advantage. That is the nature of darkened understanding.

What is gone is gone forever, and any attempt to restore the past is futile. Each day is a new day of "becoming," even if mistakes and failures mark it along the way. All manifestation is sustained daily by Adonai — God made manifest – and the miracle of life is shared across all bodies, whether mineral, vegetable, animal, or human. Grasping this truth has deep practical implications: seeing with new eyes, speaking with a different mind, and, more importantly, acting in a completely different way. This new way of seeing must come first before truly being able to do things for others, since he who seeks to heal must first have spiritual health, inspiring us to pursue it.

Those who discover a path to greater fulfillment and service to life often share simple, practical tips. A wise person can accept the suggestion and see the Magic of Light begin its work. To understand and hold onto the idea with focused attention is all that is required. Life today will reflect and grow through that attention, which can develop into a genuine and vital capacity. Therefore, instead of feeling depressed and sad, our focus should be on being cheerful and contemplating all that is beautiful and joyful, as it is too harmful to do otherwise. When unable to help where assistance is needed, a consciousness that isn't centered at the highest level cannot truly offer that help. Authentic selflessness involves sincere spiritual aspiration—the kind of dedication to Life where we consciously cooperate with Deity to activate our latent abilities to express life more fully and beautifully, especially now, with rapid changes facing us all. Isn't this an urgent matter? Is there any other way?

Of course, we all do what we can in social responsibilities and give as much as we can to support appeals, knowing that many beautiful and dedicated souls must be helped as they work in the field. However, it remains essential that understanding consciousness and undergoing periods of training are necessary so that life can be uplifted, and a very clear statement of this is truly the purpose of this work.

The magic-working Chasidim of Poland in the early 1700s would tell their unhappy and oppressed listeners that nothing closes the gates of heaven quite like a brooding and melancholy mind. Joy, however, opens the way to God's grace. No child is born without pleasure and joy, and similarly, if you want your prayers and desires to be fruitful, you must offer them with pleasure and joy.

In the pursuit of deeper initiation, it is a mistake to limit the way it can be experienced, as this would go against the idea of the unity of all life. Very high levels of relationship with the inner side of life, sometimes called the Inner School, apply to many souls who often seem like ordinary people or who sometimes visibly serve humanity. None of these are materialists; that's how they are recognized. Others have the profound privilege of studying in such an Order as this. The inner awarenesses being developed most deeply concern our current and future ability to connect with the unity of all life in a healthy and creative way. In this lies the answer to the false appearance of self-centeredness.

The most limiting factor in genuine spiritual growth is the failure to seriously implement the practical suggestions offered by those who have already walked the path. For example, if someone is brooding and melancholy, it could be said that the reasons for it are valid excuses. Every person who has become a happy, creative soul was initially very unhappy. They had to learn how to be cheerful. The Chasidim did just that. The very benevolent nature of the One Life Power will be reflected in the attention given to it.

Of course, attention also involves a basic desire. This is why the KEYS are represented in the symbolism of Tarot, and those KEYS are intended to be used to help develop specific ideas at the highest level. Key 0 always conveys the adventure of life. Key 1 supports the ability to maintain attention. Key 12 relates to reversing fixed mental patterns. Key 15 helps in seeing things as they are, not according to outward appearances, and freeing oneself from bondage leads to a rich joy of the awakened state.

Our active effort to ease the world's unhappiness by learning how to be happy ultimately leads to possessing True Happiness.

CHAPTER 12 – Savior's Birth

The Birth of the World Savior

By Paul Foster Case

The World Savior, a concept of deep mystery and significance, is the Mystical Christ, different from the Historical Jesus. According to the Gospels' account, Jesus likely was born early in October, when the Sun was in Libra.

Yet, the Church carefully connected the Festival of Christmas with the Winter Solstice. The Church inherits an ancient doctrine that predates the current church organization by thousands of years. According to this timeless Wisdom, the birth of the World Savior always takes place when the sun begins its northward journey [Winter Solstice] in the sky.

Because everything in the universe is intricately connected, the astronomical phenomena of the Winter Solstice are not just events in the sky but also serve as functions within humans, who are a microcosm or universe in miniature. This connection highlights the unity and harmony that permeate the cosmos.

Here is a clue to the practical meaning of the old tradition behind the Festival of Christmas. It's not just a historical event, but a living truth that resonates in us. Everyone has a whole zodiac. Thus, the Savior of the microcosm must also be born at the Winter Solstice, a truth that is as relevant today as it was in ancient times.

The World Savior manifests within human personality through the part of our makeup governed by the sign Capricorn. Through the influence of forces associated with this sign, we feel the initial awakening of the Liberating Power, the Royal Principle of Freedom, Christ, the Anointed One. This connection to freedom serves as a source of inspiration and strength for us all.

Thus, in Hindu astrology, the sign Capricorn is said to be the "Vahana of Vishnu" – the vehicle of the principle of preservation personified as Vishnu. Vishnu manifests as Krishna, and from Krishna came the Bhagavad Gita, proclaiming the same liberating truths attributed to Christ in the New Testament. Therefore, like the Christian Church, Hinduism testifies that what is cosmically and microcosmically represented by Capricorn is the vehicle of liberation or salvation.

The Sanskrit name for Capricorn is Makara, often translated as crocodile. Tallapragada Subba Row states that Makara means five-sided, referring to the pentagon or a figure with five sides, as well as the pentagram or five-pointed star.

Our readers understand that the pentagram symbolizes humans' control over the elements and elementals. Some of our affiliates have gained only minimal skill in the ceremonial use of this symbol. Eliphas Levi states that the pentagram represents the mysterious "athanor," the unique chemical instrument that all humans possess, through which the Great Work is achieved. Even beginners, unfamiliar with the practices I have mentioned, can see that a pentagram resembles the human body, with the head, hands, and feet corresponding to the star's five points. However, the key to all practical use of the pentagram lies in its connection to the number 5, associated with Mars, the planet whose force is exalted in Capricorn.

When an astrologer says "exalted," an alchemist understands "sublimed." Using astrological laws and forces to create physical and mental changes in human personality, a practical alchemist elevates (sublimes) the Mars force in Capricorn.

Mars rules Aries by day and Scorpio by night. Day signifies the openly expressed actions of a planetary force. Night indicates hidden actions masked by some veil or appearance. The visible manifestations of Mars in human self-awareness are through functions governed by Aries, which rules the head and brain. The hidden manifestations of Mars energy relate to functions ruled by Scorpio, which governs the reproductive organs.

The word Capricorn derives from the Latin for "goat." Around the world, goatishness signifies lust and relates to the reckless caprice typical of individuals who have not mastered the subconscious expression of the Mars force moving through Scorpio.

Thus, Capricorn, the sea goat, or Makara, the crocodile, is directly connected to the strongest urge in our subconscious. Analytical psychology refers to this drive as libido.

More analytical psychologists consider libido to be harmful to human welfare. However, Jung describes it as instinctive energy, the general force sometimes called the will to live. His student, Geraldine Coster, writes in Psycho-Analysis for Normal People: "When we so define libido, we ought to realize that we are speaking of what Christians would call The Holy Spirit."

This is precisely what the Mars force in Capricorn signifies. Capricorn is the sign of the World's Savior's birth because it frees us from all kinds of bondage, and the dominion represented by the pentagram is the libido.

Eliphas Levi clarifies this by stating that The Great Magical Agent is what man "modifies and apparently multiplies in the reproduction of his species."

Freemasonry imparts the same teaching. Every Mason is instructed that his primary goal is to master his passions. Each Mason receives a white lambskin apron, symbolizing the zodiac sign Aries, which signifies the sublimation of the Mars energy at work in Scorpio into a higher purpose within the brain. Every Mason is also given the symbol of the compasses to illustrate how the Mars energy, or the natural spontaneous drive of the passionate nature, can be controlled by intelligence.

Compasses are used to draw circles. Using them, one encircles a specific area. Circumscription represents a form of limitation, which is a characteristic of Saturn, the ruler of Capricorn. We control instinctive energy by defining an area "within which it may manifest without causing harm to ourselves or others."

In the alchemical process, this is achieved through practices that channel the Mars force via specific brain centers. These centers form the Adytum, the "Sanctum Sanctorum," or Holy of Holies, in the human temple.

According to the Masonic legend, the secret word of "Master Mason" could not be given to the builders, who rashly demanded it, because the "Sanctum Sanctorum" had not been completed. Only when the brain centers, governed by Aries, are perfected through the sublimation of the Mars force, can we hear the Word.

The Great Magical Agent and the First Matter of Alchemy are the same. That's why one alchemical treatise states the First Matter is "set up for the ruin of many and the salvation of a few."

This force is represented by Key 15 corresponding to Capricorn, "The Devil." W.E. White states: "In the eighteenth century, this card seems to have been rather a symbol of merely animal impudence." He is correct, but it should be remembered that the immodesty of animals has no evil attached to it. The feeling of shame develops in humans from misusing the Great Magical Agent, and that misuse is caused by ignorance.

When correct knowledge overcomes ignorance, and proper practice follows that knowledge, all harmful elements in innate energy are eliminated. Alongside them goes false modesty, replaced by conscious innocence, symbolized by the white apron, the Masonic emblem.

We who are on the Way of Return are working to become what the Bible describes as the State of Adam and to live in the Garden of Eden before the Fall. Yet, there is a difference. Adam and Eve, before the Fall, are symbols of "unconscious" innocence; such innocence must inevitably suffer because it is ignorant innocence. Conscious innocence cannot be tempted. It knows and understands the Great Magical Agent and cannot be deceived.

Capricorn is associated with Issachar, whom it is written: "Issachar is a strong ass, couching between two sheepfolds. And he saw that rest was good, and the earth pleasant; and bowed his shoulder to bear, and became a servant unto tribute." (Genesis 49:14.)

Issachar means "He brings reward." This aligns with the astrological doctrine regarding the tenth sign, Capricorn, and its connection to the tenth house of the horoscope, which relates to fame and the reward for successful work.

Issachar is also associated with the element linked to Capricorn, along with the inertia characteristic of that element and the planet Saturn. "And he saw that rest was good, and the earth pleasant."

Finally, we learn that Issachar became a servant. Compare this with Jesus' words: "And whoever among you may desire to become chief shall be the slave of all" (Mark 11:44).

Here is the secret of liberation. Nietzsche misunderstood it and condemned Christianity's servitude. From what is mistaken for Christianity, he was correct. But the Wisdom, hidden behind the Church's superficial doctrines, is a system of magical liberation from the chains of ignorant weakness.

This liberation is achieved by transforming forces that usually serve only their own ends into agents of "all." When these forces operate only through lower means of expression, what is harmful and evil becomes a tool for domination over the elements when their power is directed towards higher levels.

Yet the liberating power is born, or manifest, symbolized by Key 15, The Devil. Recall that Nachash, the Tempter, and Messiah, the Redeemer, are seen as two aspects of a single Reality. Thus, it is written: "The devil is God, as He is misunderstood by the wicked."

This is the most important lesson of the Winter Solstice. A lesson that most are slow to learn and often speak about glibly, as many tend to do, by repeating the words. Therefore, it is not out of place to conclude this message by reiterating the old doctrine:

> "Whatever appears to any person to be evil, inimical to his welfare, or even to what is considered to be the general welfare, is precisely the raw material for that person to work upon to achieve liberation." [1]

This applies to every situation and aspect of human life. It doesn't matter what it looks like. We may see it in ethics, diet, politics, and personal relationships. Where it shows up and how it appears are irrelevant.

What truly matters is that whenever a human observes an act, a person, or a situation that seems evil, they are seeing with ignorance rather than with the clear vision of true Wisdom. It has been said that "Beauty is in the eye of the beholder." Similarly, it can be true that "evil is in the eye of him who sees evil."

The Masters of Wisdom see good masked by appearances of wickedness, misery, and disease, and their clear vision performs miracles that bring good into active manifestation. What they do instantly, we can also accomplish, if not as quickly, by learning to bravely face whatever appears to be the face of the devil until, through "insight," we recognize God hidden behind the demon's mask.

Chapter 12 Notes

[1] Regarding the nature of evil, I want to share my thoughts. If you dance with the devil, the devil doesn't change; the devil changes you. Once you see or experience something, you can't unsee it.

That's why Ayin, the eye, is linked with Renewing Intelligence. *Through it, the Blessed Holy One rejuvenates the World of Creation.* Seeing something for the first time shifts your perspective, and your world is refreshed, for better or worse.

[2] Problems rarely disappear by ignoring them. While God is indeed hidden behind the demon's mask, it is equally true that you must act appropriately, especially in risky situations. Treating a hostile individual as a "projection" reflects poor situational awareness.

I fully agree that I am responsible for my actions and environment. That's why I steer clear of toxic people.

The spiritual truth that all humans are sparks of divinity doesn't change the reality that there are dangerous and toxic people on both physical and spiritual levels.

CHAPTER 13 – Portal Assignments

The first Portal assignment is to finish these tasks:

I confirm that I have completed items 1 through 6 listed below as part of the requirements for consideration for advancement to the Second Order. This voucher indicates that I have learned the necessary rituals (4, 5, & 6) and the signs and tokens listed in item 1, and that I can demonstrate any of them if asked. I also agree to submit my journal of Portal exercises if needed. This voucher replaces the need for an in-person interview with the Grand Chiefs.

Please initial each item and sign at the bottom of the page. The completed form must be returned to the Grand Cancellarius.

1. I have reviewed and am ready to demonstrate all Steps, Signs, Grips, Passwords, Mystic Numbers, Mystic Titles, Grand Words, and Symbols of each Grade up to and including the Portal. _____ (initials)

2. I have reviewed my obligations, emphasizing the spiritual essence of genuine loving humility, the spirit of true sacrifice through service to the ONE in all my efforts, a sense of what in my nature truly helps to redeem, as well as the levels of genuine compassion I have cultivated that help to extend the divine light.
_____

3. I will submit my Journal of Portal Exercises to the Grand Praemonstrator if requested. _____

4. I have learned and can perform the Greater Invoking and Banishing Ritual of Water. _____

5. I have learned and can perform the formula of The Awakening of the Palaces of Equilibrium and know the three formulas for the circulation of force. _____

6. I have learned and can perform the Ritual of the Flaming Cube. _____

Then there is a series of papers to write, each of which takes a month.

First Paper – Ray of Power

You have become familiar with the three rays of Power, Wisdom, and Love through your studies and experiences in the First Order Grades. In the Grade of Zelator, you were asked to write a paper on the Three Mothers as an initial step in exploring the rays. Now, as a 4=7 Major, you have gained further understanding of the rays as you advanced through the Grades.

Please write a paper about the Ray of Power as you understand it now. This paper will be based on your current meditative exploration of the Power Ray and the insights you've gained. Use your Three Mothers Paper and past meditations, notes, etc., as a starting point for your present understanding. There is no required length for this paper, but ensure it accurately reflects your understanding. The paper should be typed or written on a computer, and please keep a copy for yourself, as it will not be returned.

The paper must be submitted to the Praemonstrator on or before 28 days after receiving this assignment. (In other words, you have 28 days to complete the assignment.)

Also, until your advancement, you will perform the *Ritual of Awakening the Palaces of Equilibrium*.

Second Paper – Ray of Wisdom

Continuing your review of the Three Rays, write a paper on the Wisdom Ray based on current meditations and understanding. This meditative paper incorporates insights and perceptions from your present viewpoint as a 4=7 Major.

Third Paper – Ray of Love

Please write a paper on the Ray of Love based on current meditations on the Love Ray. As before, this is a meditative paper incorporating insights and understanding from your present viewpoint as a 4=7 Major.

Fourth Paper – Unreserved Dedication

You are asked to write a paper focusing on your understanding and the personal significance of the Unreserved Dedication provided in the 4=7 Grade of Philosophus, using this document as the stimulus for your assignment. Feel free to choose any style you prefer (explanatory, reflective, commentary, meditative, etc.).

Fifth Paper – Alchemical Meditations

Prepare a paper presenting your interpretation of the alchemical diagrams in either (a.) Splendor Solis or (b.) Liber Mutus. This should be a meditative exercise focused on the illustrations, not a commentary on the text.

CHAPTER 14 – 4 = 7 to Portal

Preparation for the Passage from 4=7 to Portal

This paper is to be given to the Philosophus by the examining Chief after completing the examination to pass from Philosophus to the Portal of the Vault of the Adept.

The Philosophus should complete the following preparation during the time between the examination and the Portal ritual. There will be no exam on this material; however, the work outlined here is an important preparation for what is to come.

Incense is optional. If used, it should be Frankincense.

The 26th Path of Ayin

Set before you the 15th Trump, The Devil. Please focus on it with a calm, alert, and receptive mindset. Spend one week practicing this simple meditation every day.

The 24th Path of Nun

Repeat the first practice but with the 13th Trump, Death. Spend one week practicing this simple meditation daily. (The sequence of these meditations is precise and important. Do not perform the meditations in the order of the Tarot Keys, but rather in the sequence provided here.)

Repeat the second practice, but with the 14th Trump, Temperance. Spend one week practicing this simple meditation daily.

The Doctrines of the Grade of 4=7 Major (Portal)

Netzach is linked to the Occult (hidden) Intelligence. The Hebrew word for hidden is Nesether (נסתר). These letters correspond to the Tarot Keys: Death, Temperance, The World, and The Sun.

Set out these Tarot Keys from right to left for this meditation. From each is derived a doctrine, or initiatory truth, corresponding to the Grade you are preparing to enter. These doctrines are as follows:

Nun, Death: The dissolution of form is a core aspect of the Cosmic process. All things undergo change. All conditions fade away. No form ever remains permanent. Existence is a continuous flow, a series of waves, an eternal movement.

Samekh, Temperance: Every person is directly guided by the One Identity. Each personal action is a unique expression of that One Identity's influence. Knowing this is the key to the complete freedom of the truly wise.

Tav, The World: All form is a limitation of the infinite energy of the Life Power. The primary cause of limitation is the image-making power of the Universal Mind. Every act of human imagination is a specific expression of this image-making power through a personal center. Therefore, human imagination is, in essence though not in degree, the same as the Imagination that creates the Universe.

Resh, The Sun: Human personality is a synthesis of all cosmic processes. Man summarizes everything that came before him and serves as the starting point for creating a New Creature. The natural man is the seed of the spiritual man.

Lay out these four Tarot Trumps as usual for each day's meditation. Choose one of the cards and focus on it for several minutes so it can convey its message to your subconscious. Then, use the Doctrine corresponding to the card as the key to the rest of your meditation.

Keep practicing these until the date of the Portal Ritual.

PAUL FOSTER CASE BOOKS

1. SEVEN STEPS IN PRACTICAL OCCULTISM

2. AN INTRODUCTION TO THE TAROT AND ASTROLOGY

3. TAROT FUNDAMENTALS

4. TAROT INTERPRETATIONS

5. THE MASTER PATTERN

6. THE THIRTY-TWO PATHS OF WISDOM

7. THE TREE OF LIFE

8. THE NEOPHYTE RITUALS OF PAUL FOSTER CASE

9. THE ATTUNEMENT RITUALS OF PAUL FOSTER OF CASE

10. THE SECOND ORDER RITUALS OF PAUL FOSTER CASE

11. THE NEOPHYTE GRADE WORK OF PAUL FOSTER CASE.

12. THE ZELATOR GRADE WORK OF PAUL FOSTER CASE.

13. THE THEORICUS GRADE WORK OF PAUL FOSTER CASE.

14. THE PRACTICUS GRADE WORK OF PAUL FOSTER CASE.

WADE COLEMAN BOOKS

1. SEPHER SAPPHIRES Volume 1

2. SEPHER SAPPHIRES Volume 2

3. THE ASTROLOGY WORKBOOK

4. MAGIC OF THE PLANETS

5. THE ZODIAC OF DENDARA EGYPT

6. THE MAGICAL PATH

7. ATHANASIUS KIRCHER'S QUADRIVIUM

To contact the author,

DENDARA_ZODIAC(at)protonmail.com